THE
VAN HALEN
ANTHOLOGY

Management: E.L. Management
Music Engraving by W.R. Music
Production: Daniel Rosenbaum/Rana Bernhardt
Art Direction: Rosemary Cappa-Jenkins/Jim Darling
Director of Music: Mark Phillips

CONTENTS

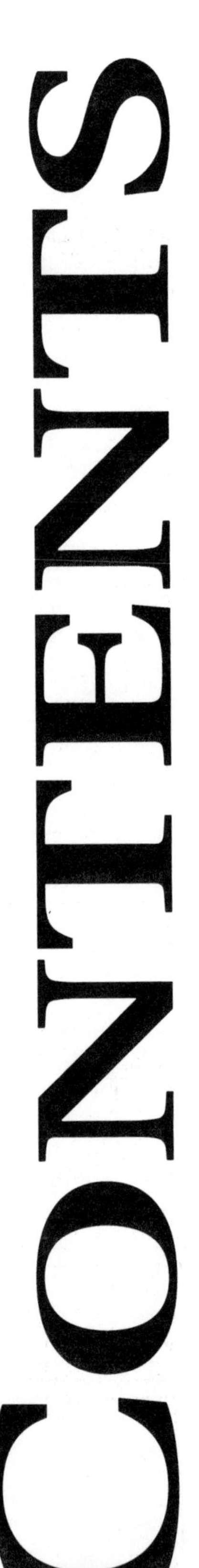

RUNNIN' WITH THE DEVIL

Words and Music by
Edward Van Halen, Alex Van Halen,
Michael Anthony and David Lee Roth

C/ED/E
G/EA/E E
1st Verse
A5
G/A
F#m/A
Em/A
I live my life like there's no to-mor-row,
(end Rhy. Fig. 1)
H
Rhy. Fig. 2
H
sl.
mf
sl.
*Lightly palm mute staccatoed notes.
A5
G/A
F#m Em
A5
G/A
and all I've got I had to steal.
Least I don't need to
Harm.
(8va)
sl.
let ring
Harm.
**Open G stg. sounds with harmonic.
F#m/A
Em/A
A5
G/A
F#m/A Em/A
Em
beg or bor-row.
Yes, I'm liv-in' at a pace that kills.
(end Rhy. Fig. 2)
sl.
f
*Strum backwards from high to low. sl.
*Chorus
w/Rhy. Fig. 1
C/E D/E
G/E A/E E
C/E D/E
Run-nin' with the dev-il.
*w/lead voc. ad lib
G/E A/E E
C/E D/E
G/E A/E E
Run-nin' with the dev-

2nd Verse
w/Rhy. Fill 1
w/Rhy. Fig. 2
C/E D/E
G/E A/E E
A5
G/A
F#m/A
Em/A
il.
I found the sim-ple life ain't so sim-ple
A5
G/A
Substitute Rhy. Fill 2
F#m Em
Resume Rhy. Fig. 2
A5
G/A
when I jumped out on that road.
I got no love, no
F#m/A
Em/A
A5
G/A
F#m/A
Em/A
Em
love you'd call real.
Ain't got no-bod-y wait-in' at home.
*Chorus
w/Rhy. Fig. 1
C/E D/E
G/E A/E E
C/E D/E
G/E A/E E
*w/lead voc. ad lib
Run-nin' with the dev - il.
C/E D/E
G/E A/E E
C/E D/E
w/Rhy. Fill 3
G/E A/E E
Run-nin' with the dev - il.
Gtr. II
sl.
w/echo & reverb
14
7 14
sl.
Rhy. Fill 1
H
H
sl.
sl.
mf
7 8 10 9
7 9 9
7 9 11 9
9
9
9
*Roll down gtr. volume
slightly w/vol. knob.
Rhy. Fill 2
tr
sl.
tr
2 0
7
4 2
7
(5)
sl.
*Trill double stop
on 2nd & 3rd stgs.
Rhy. Fill 3 (Gtr. I)
H
sl. sl.
H
7 8 10 9
7 9 9
7 9 11 9
17
sl. sl.

Guitar solo I
A5
Gtr. I
Gtr. II
pick slides
G5
⑥12fr.
E
sl.
P
P.M.
sl. sl.
P
P
sl. sl.
sl. sl.
sl. sl.
A5
pick slide
G5
E5
⑥17fr.
A
Full
1/2Full
P
sl.
P
sl.
Full
P
1/2Full
sl.
sl.
P
sl.
C/E
D/E
G/E
A/E
E
Whoo!
Rhy. Fig. 3
H
sl. sl.
H
sl. sl.
C/E
D/E
G/E
A/E
E
You know, I,
H
sl.
H
sl.

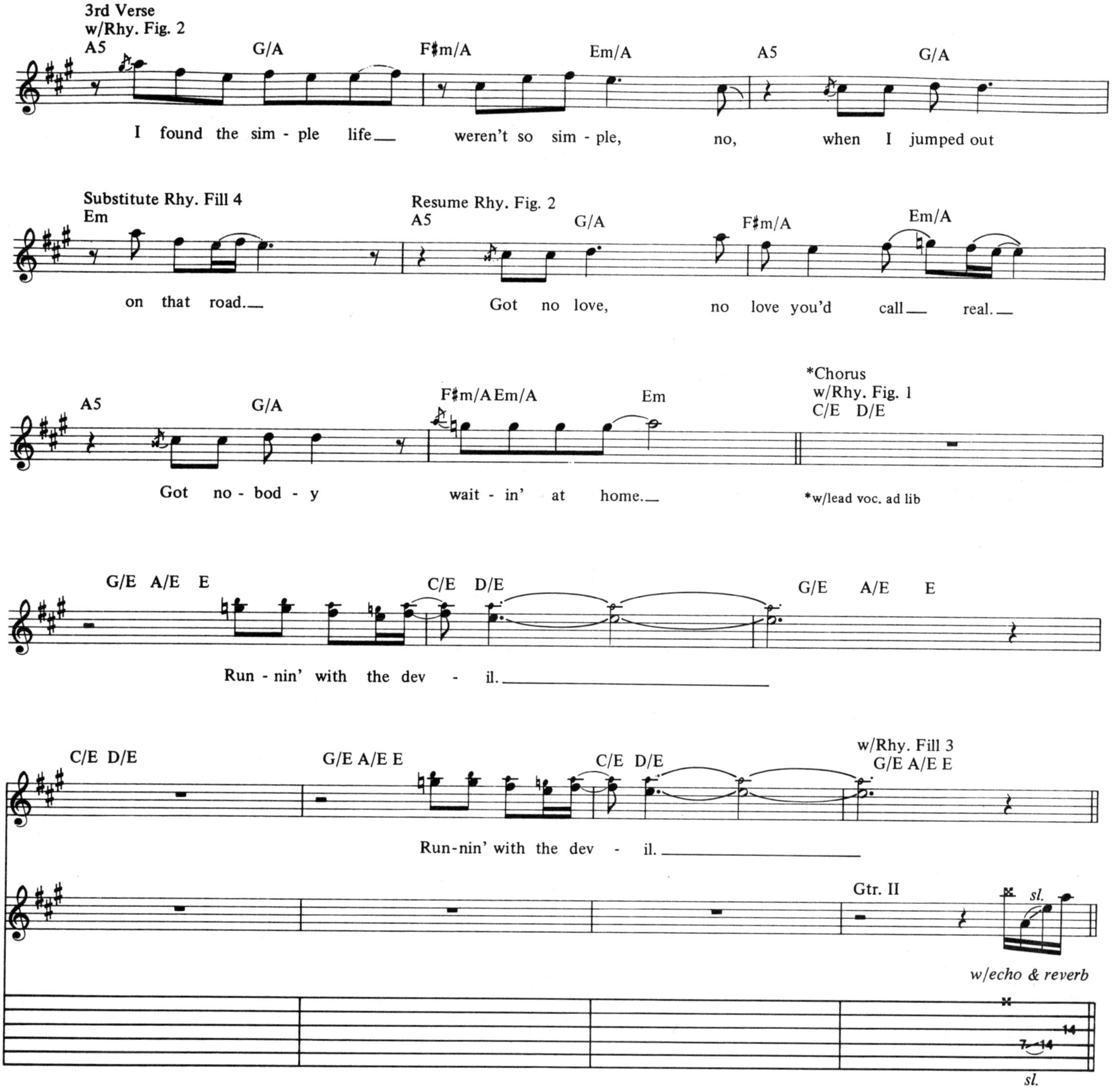

3rd Verse
w/Rhy. Fig. 2
A5 G/A F♯m/A Em/A A5 G/A
I found the sim - ple life___ weren't so sim - ple, no, when I jumped out
Substitute Rhy. Fill 4
Em
Resume Rhy. Fig. 2
A5 G/A F♯m/A Em/A
on that road.___ Got no love, no love you'd call___ real.___
A5 G/A F♯m/A Em/A Em
*Chorus
w/Rhy. Fig. 1
C/E D/E
Got no - bod - y wait - in' at home.___
*w/lead voc. ad lib
G/E A/E E C/E D/E G/E A/E E
Run - nin' with the dev - il.
C/E D/E G/E A/E E C/E D/E
w/Rhy. Fill 3
G/E A/E E
Run-nin' with the dev - il.
Gtr. II
sl.
w/echo & reverb
14
7 14
sl.

Rhy. Fill 4
Harm.
(8va)
let ring
Harm.
12
7 5 5
0
2
5
12 7 5

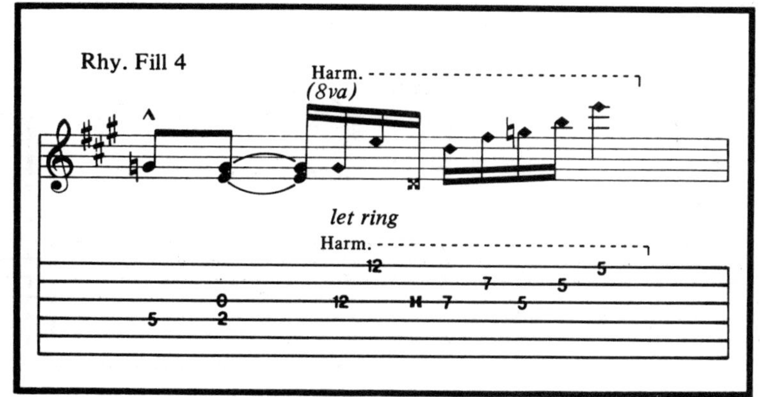

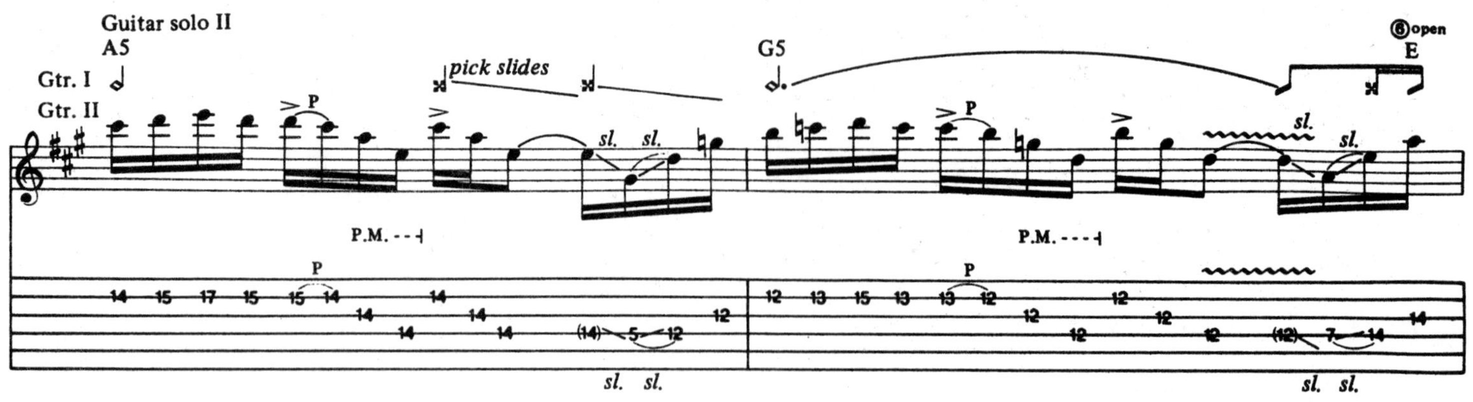

Guitar solo II
A5
Gtr. I
Gtr. II
pick slides
G5
⑥open
E
P
P
sl. sl.
sl.
P.M.
P.M.
14 15 17 15 15 14 14
14 14 12
14 14 (14) 5 12
P
12 13 15 13 13 12 12 12
12 12 12
12 (12) 7 14
sl. sl.
sl. sl.

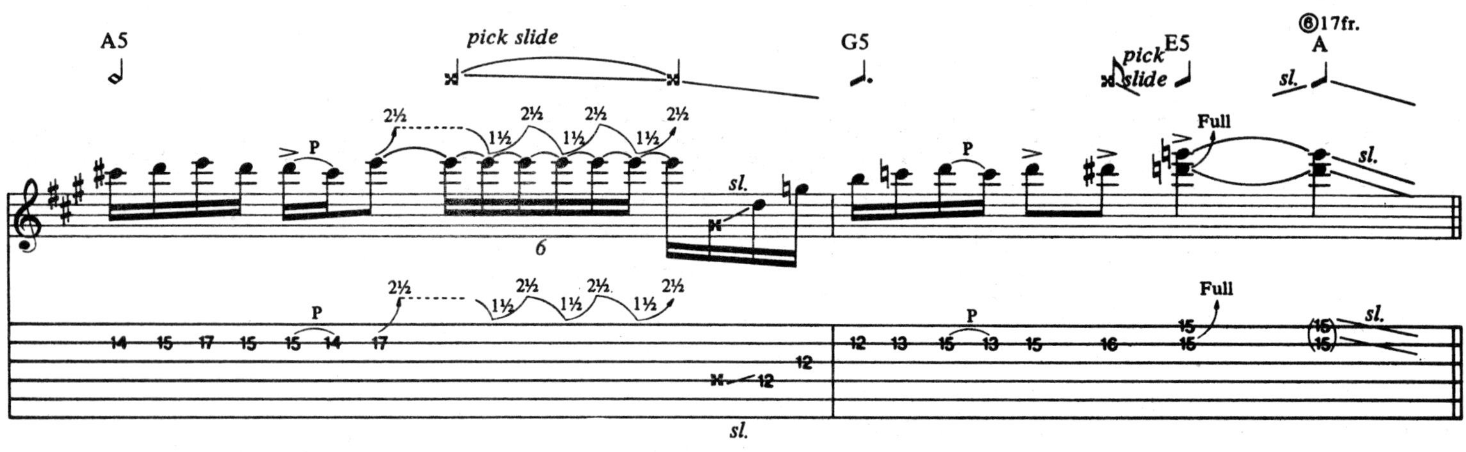

A5
pick slide
G5
pick slide
E5
⑥17fr.
A
Full
2½ 2½ 2½ 2½
1½ 1½ 1½ 1½
sl.
P
P
sl.
6
2½ 2½ 2½ 2½
1½ 1½ 1½
Full
sl.
14 15 17 15 15 14 17
12
P
12 13 15 13 15 16 15
15 (15)
(15)
12
sl.

*Out-chorus
w/Rhy. Fig. 3 (4½ times)
C/E D/E
G/E A/E E
C/E D/E
Run - nin' with the dev - il.
*w/lead voc. ad lib till end

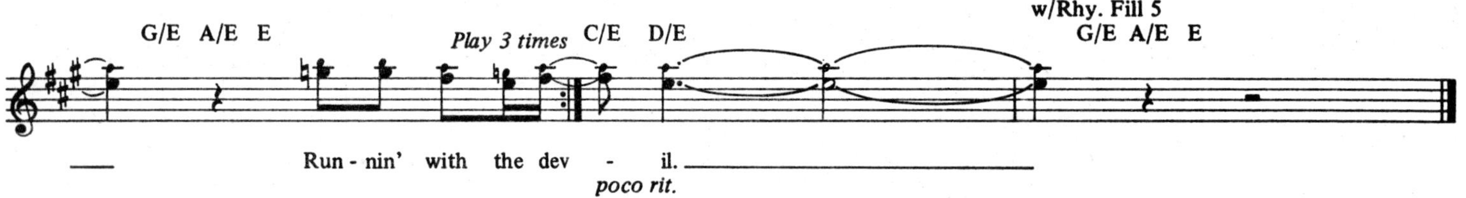

G/E A/E E
Play 3 times
C/E D/E
w/Rhy. Fill 5
G/E A/E E
Run - nin' with the dev - il.
poco rit.

Rhy. Fill 5
H
sl.
H
sl.
7 8 10 9 (9)
7 9 9 (9)
7 9 11 9 (9)

ERUPTION

Music by
Edward Van Halen, Alex Van Halen,
Michael Anthony and David Lee Roth

Tune down 1/2 step:
⑥ = Eb ③ = Gb
⑤ = Ab ② = Bb
④ = Db ① = Eb

Free time (♩ = 92)

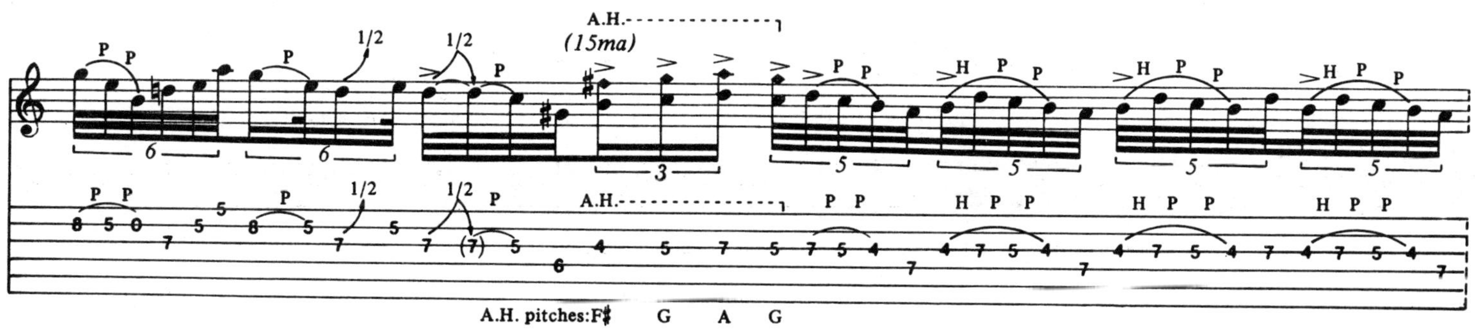

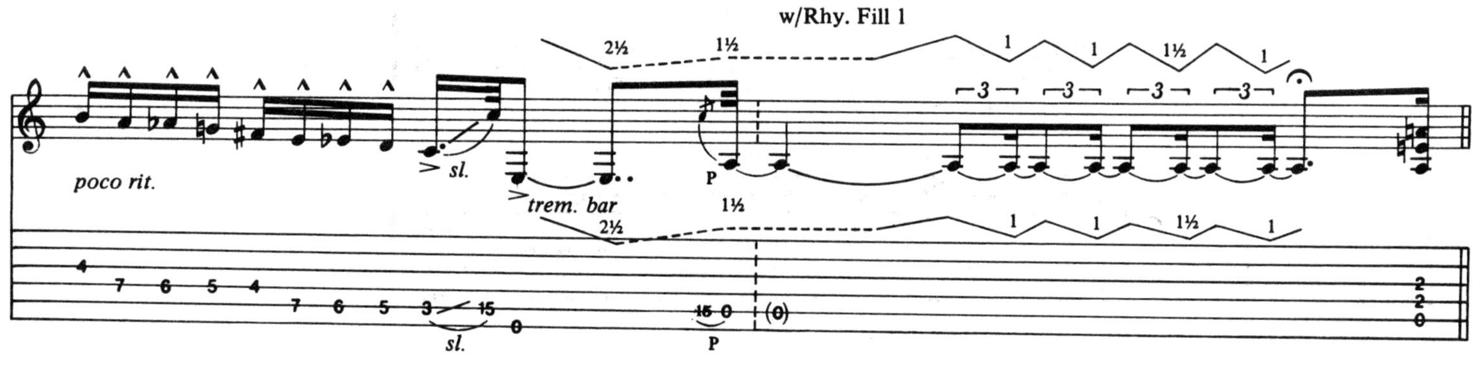

9

8va-
Full
A5
G5
D5
sl.
Harm.
*Release finger pressure when arriving at 19fr. at end
of slide to sound F# natural harmonic.
8va-
Faster (♩ = 132)
loco
trem. bar
accel.
rake
8va-
Rhy. Fill 1
Overdubbed gtr.

loco
sl.
3:2
1/2
trem. bar
dim.
*w/more intense flanging.
ff sl.
P.M.
tr
rake
(trills)
Faster (♩ = 146)
(C#m)
poco rit.
poco accel.
*w/flanger (slow sweep, medium intensity & regeneration)
& tape echo delay (approx. 150 ms. w/one repeat).
(A)
(A dim)
(B)
*Slightly rushed.

*Slightly rushed.
(Echoplex on)
*Harm.
Fdbk.
1/4
trem. bar
rit.
dim.
**w/tape echo effect.
Fdbk. pitch: B
*Tap open low E at 12fr.
to produce octave harmonic.
**Univox tape echo runaway feedback effect.

AIN'T TALKIN' 'BOUT LOVE

Words and Music By
Edward Van Halen, Alex Van Halen,
Michael Anthony and David Lee Roth

Gtr. I plays Fill 1 2nd time
N.C.
Am
F5
G5
N.C.
Yeah, you may have all you want, __ ba - by, __ but I got some-thin' you need, __
Oh yeah, you think you're real - ly cook-in', ba - by. __ you bet - ter find your-self a
P.M.
H
P.M.
H
Am
F5
G5
N.C.
Gtr. I plays Fill 2 2nd time
Chorus
Am
G
friend.
oh yeah. __
My friend. __
Ain't talk - in' 'bout love. __
P.M.
sl.
pick slides
P.M.
P.M.
*Play cue note 2nd time.
N.C.
Am
G5
N.C.
Am
G
My love is rot - ten to the core. __
Ain't talk - in' 'bout love.
P.M.
H
P.M. P.M. P.M.
P.M.
H
P.M. P.M. P.M.
H
H
Fill 1
A.H.
(8va)
P.M.
A.H.
H
Fill 2
pick sl. (steady gliss.)
sl.
sl.

14

Gtr I plays Fill 3 2nd time
1.
N.C.
Am
G
N.C.
Just like I told you be - fore, ___ yeah, be - fore. ___ You know you're sem - i good -
P.M.
H
P.M.
H
2.
Am
G
Guitar solo I
**Am
G5
___ be - fore, ___ uh, be - fore ___ uh, be - fore ___ be - fore.
P.M. P.M. P.M.
let ring
sl.
sl.
*Doubled by
elec. sitar (Gtr.II).
**Chords implied by bass line.
w/Fill 4
Am
sl.
sl.
G5
sl.
sl.
†trem bar
sl.
sl.
sl.
sl.
sl.
sl.
sl.
sl.
†Gtr. I only (Gtr. II sim. figure w/o trem. bar).
Fill 3
Full
sl.
trem. bar
Full
sl.
P
*Hold bend
while sliding.
P
Fill 4
sl.
sl.
sl.
sl.
sl.
sl.

Ain't talk-in' 'bout-a love.
Babe, it's-a rot-ten to the core.
Ain't talk-in' 'bout love.
Just like I told you be-fore,
Fill 5
Gtr. II
hold bend
grad. release

3rd Verse
Am   G   Am   F5   G5   N.C.
uh, be - fore.___ I been to the edge,___ an' there I stood an' looked
P.M. P.M.   P.M.
*Dim. w/vol. control.
mp
(flanger off)
P.M.
let ring

Am   F5   G5   N.C.   Am   F5   G5   N.C.
down.___ You know I lost a lot of friends___ there,___ ba - by, I got no time to mess a -
P.M.   let ring   let ring

Am   F5   G5   N.C.   Am   G
round. (exhale) Mmm,___ so if you want it, got to bleed for it, ba - by. Yeah, got to, got to
sim.   P.M.   P   P.M.   f   mp   let ring
Harm.
(8va)
*w/flanger
*Flanger set to sweep upper partial harmonics.

Am   G   Am   G
bleed, ba - by. Mmm,___ you got to, got to bleed, ba - by. Hey, got to, got to
Harm.   Harm.
(8va)   (8va)
let ring   let ring
f   mp   f   mp
Harm.   Harm.

Am   G   Chorus Am   G   N.C.
bleed, ba - by.__   Ain't talk - in' 'bout love.   My love is rot - ten to the
Harm. (8va)   Harm. (8va)
mp   let ring   *cresc.   f sl.
H
Harm.   Harm.
*Increase volume w/vol. control.
sl.

Am   G5   N.C.   Am   G   N.C.
core.__   Ain't talk - in' 'bout love.   Just like I told you be - fore,
sl. sl. sl. sl.
trem. bar
P.M. P.M. P.M.   P.M. P.M. P.M.   P.M.
H
sl. sl. sl. sl.

Am   G   Am   G   N.C.
be - fore, be - fore.__   Ain't talk - in' 'bout love.   Don't wan-na talk a - bout
P.M.   P.M.   P.M. P.M. P.M.   P.M.
H   H   H   H

Am   G5   N.C.   Am   G5   N.C.
love.   Don't need to talk a - bout love.   Ain't gon - na talk a - bout
8va
Full   Full   Full   loco
hold bend   pick sl.
P.M. P.M. P.M.   P.M. P.M.   P.M.
Full   Full   Full   sl.
H

Am
G5
Guitar solo II
**Am
G5
love.
No more,
no more.
Ah!
P.M.
P.M.
P.M.
sl.
*Doubled
by Gtr. II.
**Chords implied by bass.
sl.
sl.
sl.
sl.
1/2
1
1
sl.
Am
sl.
G5
sl.
sl.
†trem. bar
1/2
1
1
sl.
sl.
sl.
sl.
† Gtr. I only (Gtr. II sim. figure w/o trem. bar).
w/Fill 6
Am
sl.
G5
P
sl.
sl.
H
P
H
P
H
P
Am
G5
sl.
sl.
sl.
sl.
sl.
P
H
P
H
P
H
P
sl.
sl.
Out-chorus
Am
G5
Hey!
Hey!
Hey!
Hey!
Hey!
Hey!
Full
P
5
Full
P.M.
P.M.
P.M.
Full
trem. bar
5
H
Fill 6
(Gtr. II)
sl.
sl.
sl.
sl.
Full
Full
grad. release
sl.
sl.
Full
Full
sl.
sl.

Am
G5
Am
G5
Hey! Hey! Hey!
Hey! Hey! Hey!
P.M. P.M. P.M.
P.M.
H
Full Full Full
sl.
Full Full Full sl.
Am
G5
Am
G5
Play 4 times
Hey! Hey! Hey!
Hey! Hey! Hey!
P.M. P.M. P.M.
P.M.
H
H
P.M. P.M. P.M.
sl.
sl.
Outro
A5
B5
C
A5
B5
E5
sl.
sl. sl. P
trem. bar
sl.
sl. sl. P
6
Am
B5
C5
hold bar down
sl.
sl.
sl.
sl.
A5
B5
Em7
Free time
E9
2½
sl.
6
trem. bar
sl. P
P.M.
6
2½
sl.
sl. P
*Fret chord with trem. bar partially depressed, strike
chord, quickly return bar to pitch and slide chord shape
down in fast gliss.

FEEL YOUR LOVE TONIGHT

Words and Music by
Edward Van Halen, Alex Van Halen,
Michael Anthony and David Lee Roth

21

A5
D/A
A5
D/A
N.C.(E7)
C
F#5
B5
N.C.(E7)
yes. Uh, too, too far. Uh, so I,
I told the fel-las out be-hind the bar. So let me tell you, hon-ey, just how fine you are,
yes. I guess you are. You see I'm beg-gin' you, please,
(Beg-gin' you, ba-by, beg-gin' on my bend-ed knees.) on my knees. Say-in' I
P.M.
sl.
T
P
*Hold B5 chord shape
while tapping-on and
sliding with R.H.

Chorus
can't wait to feel your love to - night. Ooh!
P.M. P.M. P.M. P.M. P.M.
1/2 P 1/2 P P P 1/2 P P
2nd Verse
A5 D/A A5 D/A
Seen you driv - in' up and down my road. I tell you, hon - ey, you're the
1/2 semi-harm. P
N.C.(E7)
pret - ti - est girl I know, yes. Uh, that's for sure.
P.M. P.M. P.M. P.M. P.M. P.M. P.M. P.M. P.M.
A5 D/A A D/A
But, uh, bet - ter use it up be - fore it gets old. No. I tell you, hon - ey, now you've
P.M. P.M. P.M.

N.C.(E7)
let your life grow cold, no. Uh, no, no, no.
P.M. P.M. P.M. P.M. - - -
sl.
C
F#5
B5
I'm-a beg-gin' you, on my knees.
(Beg - gin' you, ba - by, beg - gin' on my bend - ed knees.)
P.M. P.M. P.M. - - - - - - - -
T sl. T sl.
*Hold B5 chord shape
while tapping-on and
sliding with R.H.
Chorus
E5 A/E D5/E A/E D5 E5 A/E D5/E
w/Rhy. Fig. 1 (2½ times)
I can't wait to feel your love to - night.
(I can't wait to feel
Rhy. Fig. 1
(end Rhy. Fig. 1)
Fdbk. P.M. P.M. P.M. P.M. - - - P.M. P.M. P.M.
sl. sl.
A/E D5 E5 A/E D5/E A/E D5 E5 A/E D5/E
I can't wait to feel your love to - night.
your love to - night.) (I can't wait. I

3rd Verse
A/E   D5   E5 A5   D/A   A5
Whoo!   Well, I been work-in' since-a ten of nine.
can't   wait.)
P.M.   sl.   sl.   P   sl.
D/A   N.C.(E7)
I'll tell you, sug-ar, by mid-night I'll be fly'n',
P.M.   P.M.   P.M.   P.M.   P.M.
sl.   sl.   sl.
A5
fly-in' high.   Whoo!
P.M.   P.M.   P.M.   P.M.   rake   1½   Full   1½   sl.
A   D/A   A5   D/A
We'll hit the town. We'll have a hell of a time.   I'll tell you, hon-ey, by
P   sl.   sl.   P   P.M.   sl.   sl.

N.C.(E7)
morn - ing you'll be mine, ___ yes, _______ all mine. ___
sl.
P.M. P.M. P.M. P.M. P.M.
C
You know I'm beg - gin' you, ba - by.
(Beg - gin' you, ba - by,
P.M. P.M. P.M. P.M. P.M. P.M.
sl.
F#5 B5 E5
I'm on my knees. _______________ I ___
beg - gin' on my bend - ed knees.)
Fdbk. P.M.
Fdbk. pitches: F# & B
Chorus
w/Rhy. Fig. 1 (3½ times)
A/E D5/E A/E D5 E5 A/E D5/E A/E D5 E5
___ can't wait to feel ___ your love to - night. ___
(I ___ can't wait to feel ___ your love to - night.) ___

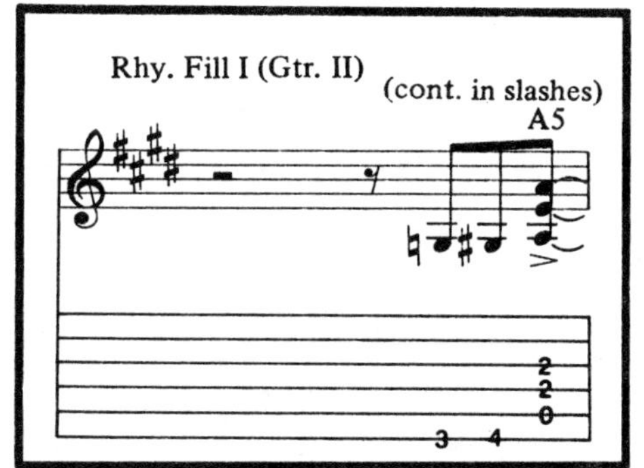

Rhy. Fill I (Gtr. II)
(cont. in slashes)
A5

C#5 C5 B5 A5
A A6
A5 A
P.M.
P.M.
Full Full Full
1/2
P
P P
1/2
sl.
sl.
Full Full
sl.
3 3
6
6
3
trem. pick
Full Full Full
1/2
P
P P
1/2
sl.
sl.
Full Full
sl.
A A6
A5 E E5
E6 E E5
E5(type 2) E5
E5(type 2) E6
E5(type 2) E5
C5
P.M.
P.M.
P.M.
sl.
Full Full
sl.
2
3
3
Full
semi-harm.
P
P
1/4
sl.
Full Full
sl.
2
Full
P
P
1/4
sl.
sl. D5
B5
w/Rhy. Fill 2
E5
Full
Full
semi-harm.
semi-harm.
rake
sl.
Fdbk.
I
Full
Full
Fdbk. pitch: F#
Rhy. Fill 2
B5
(Gtr. II out)
E5
T sl.
sl.
sl.
Fdbk.
T sl.
sl.
sl.
Fdbk. pitches: B & F#

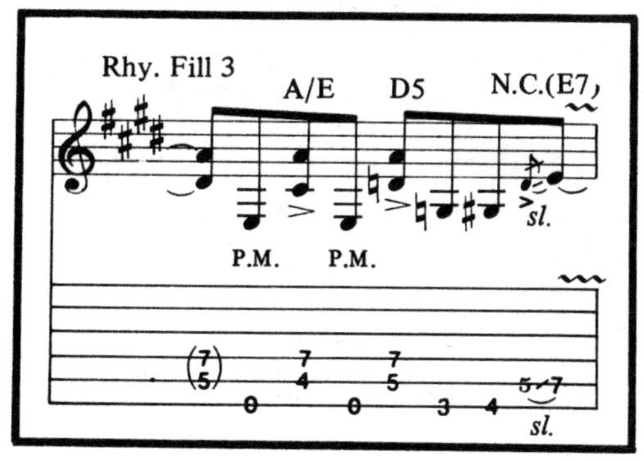
Rhy. Fill 3
A/E   D5   N.C.(E7)
P.M.   P.M.

SPANISH FLY

Music by Edward Van Halen,
Alex Van Halen, Michael Anthony
and David Lee Roth

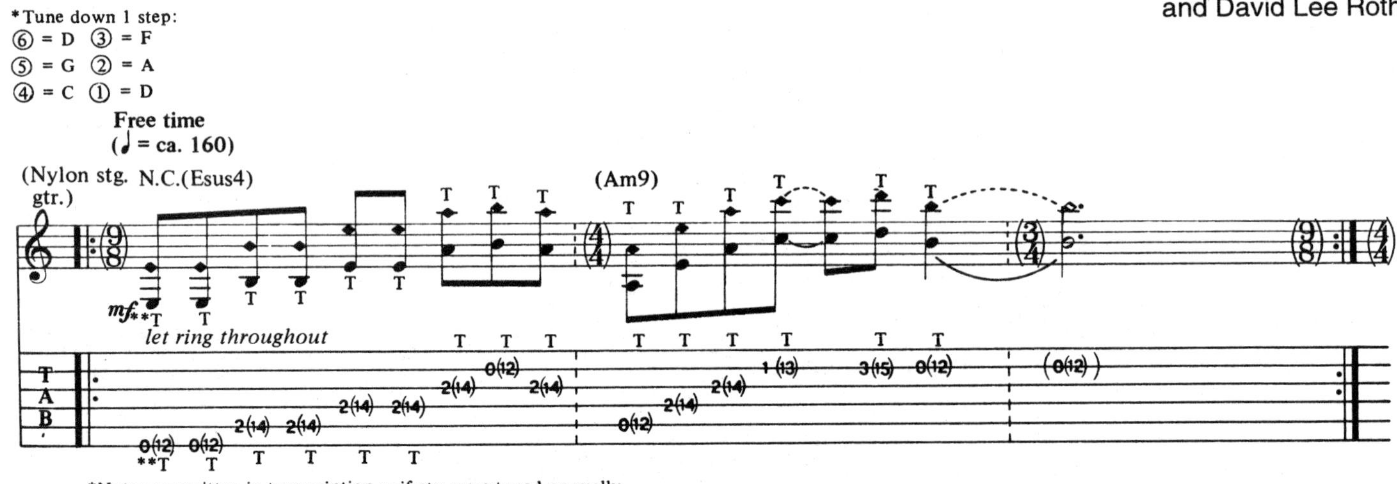

*Notes are written in transcription as if gtr. were tuned normally.
Tapped harmonics. Hold chord forms and tap stgs. at frets indicated in **parentheses.

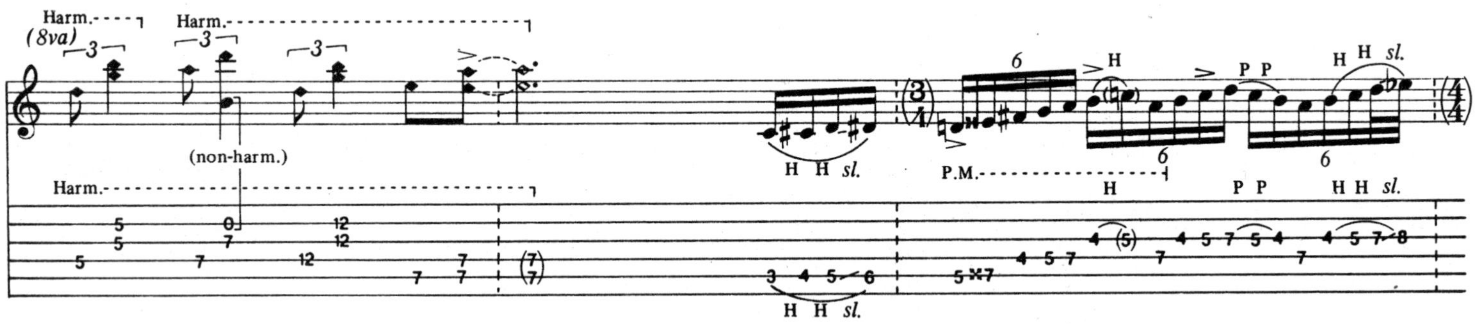

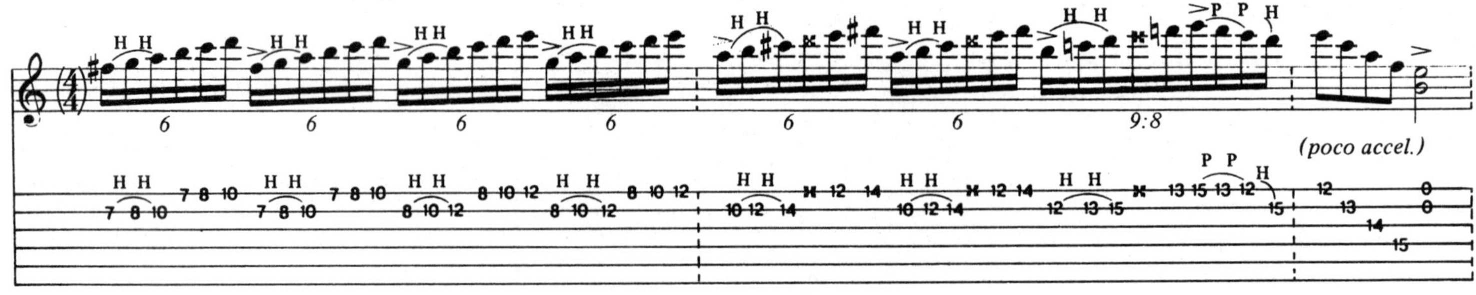

Copyright © 1979 Van Halen Music (ASCAP)
International Copyright Secured All Rights Reserved

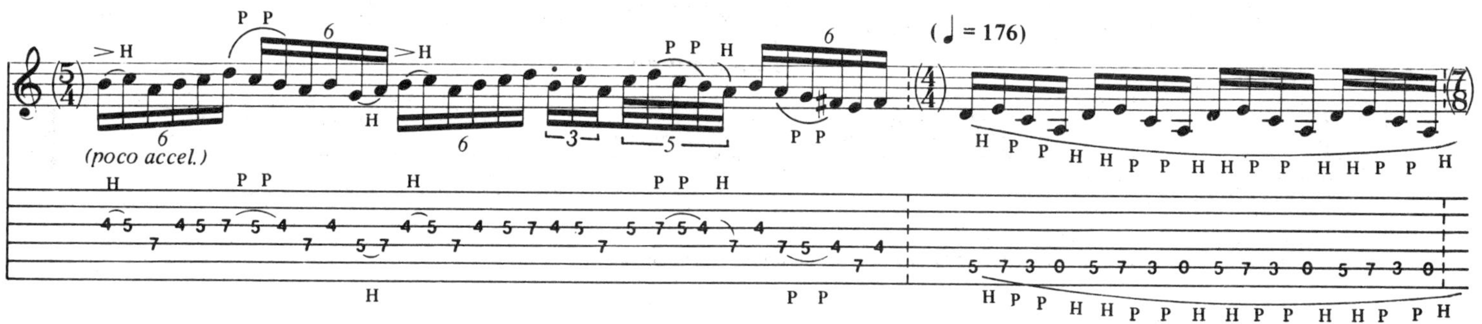
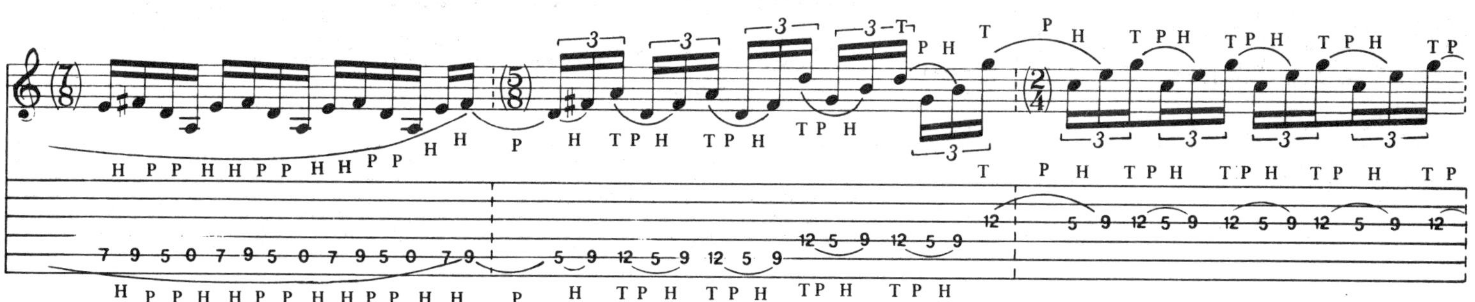
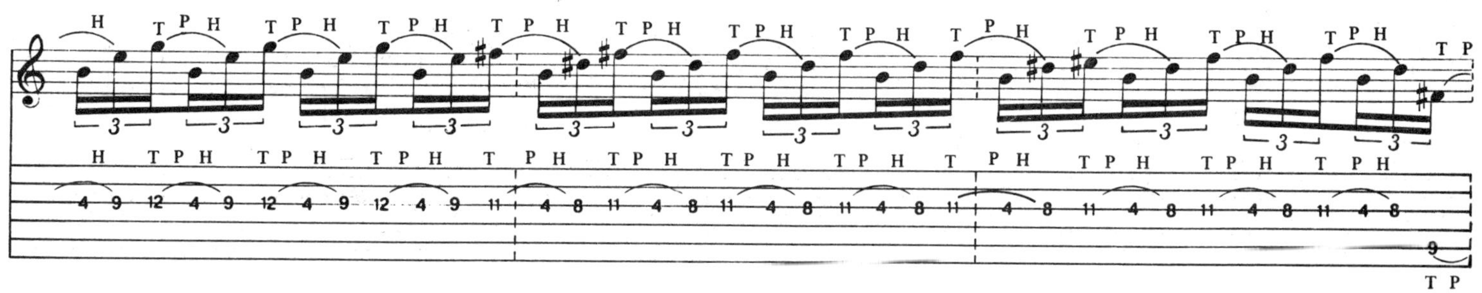
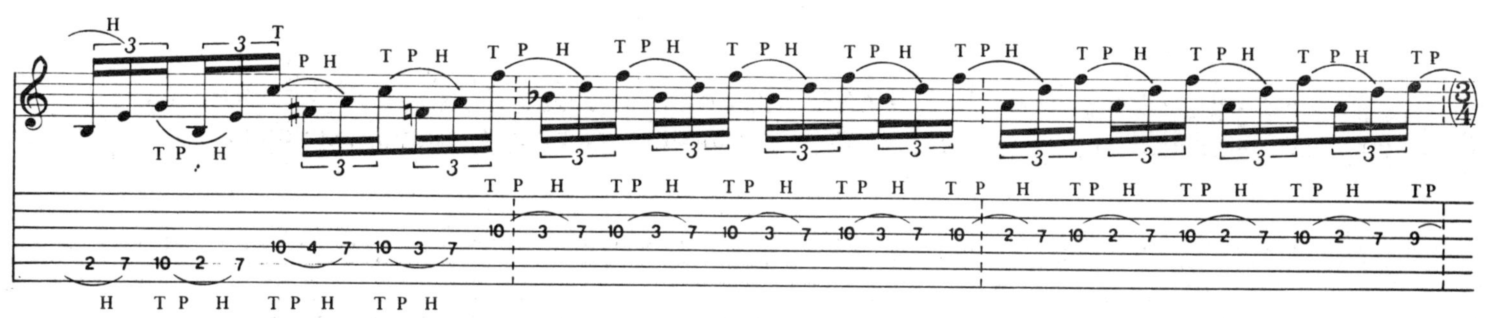

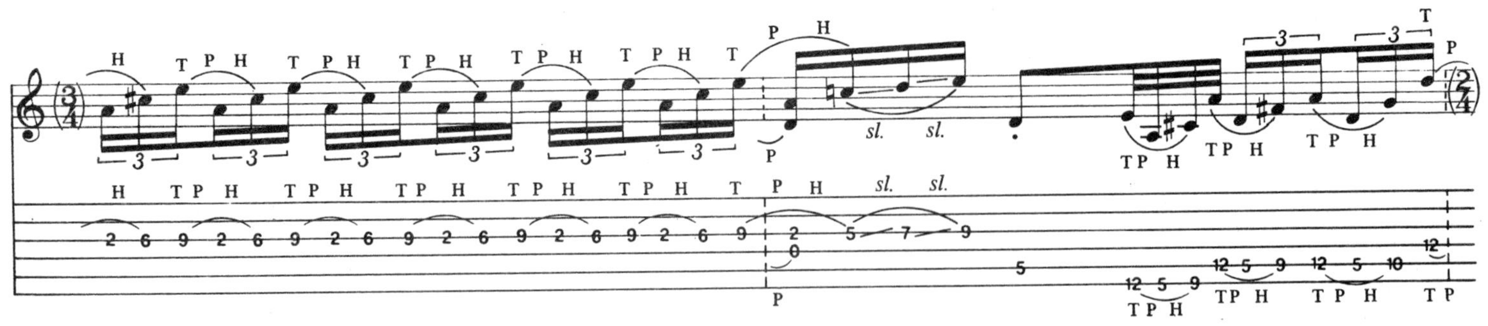

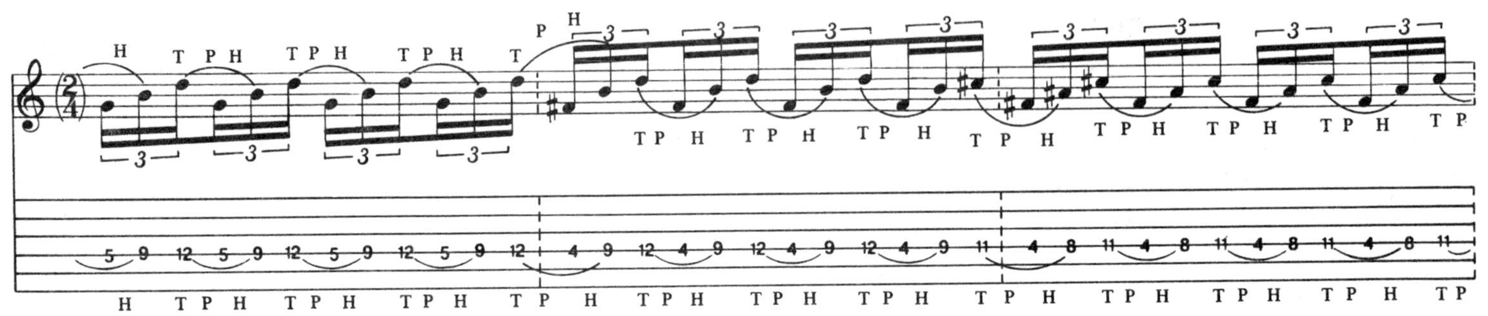

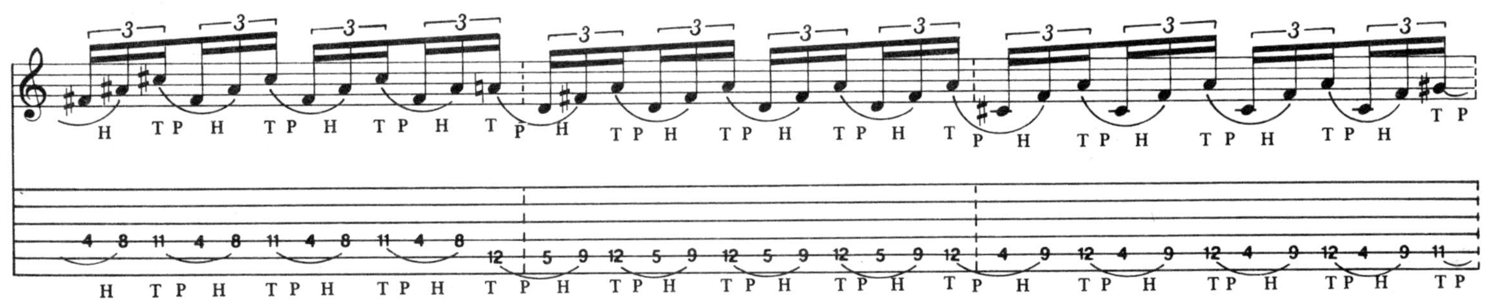

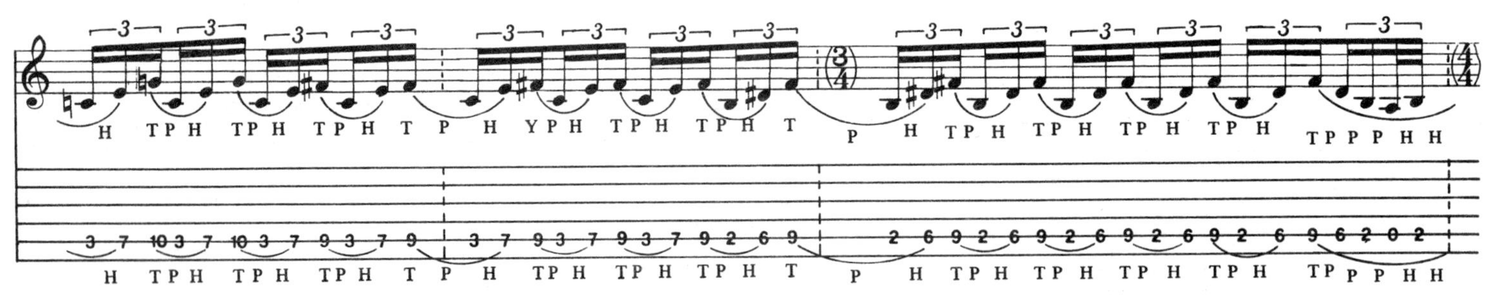

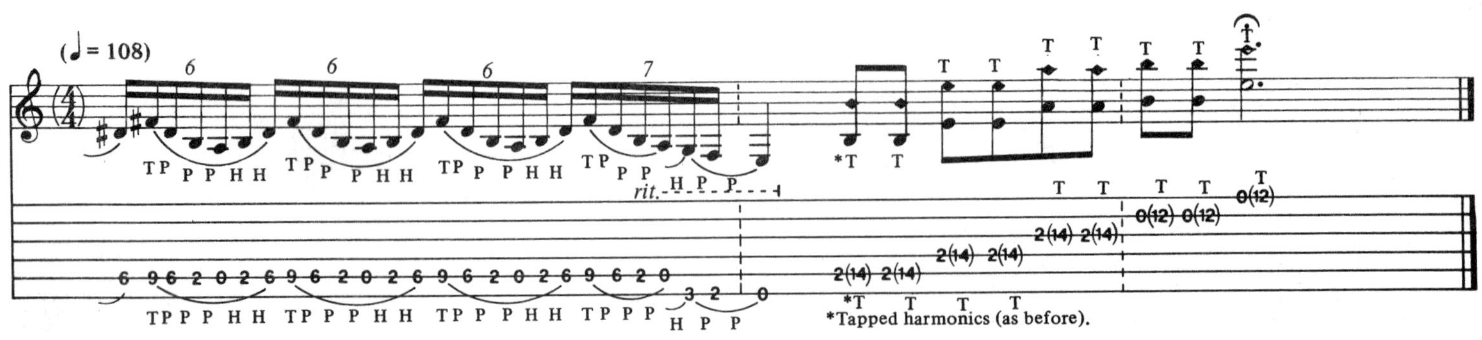
*Tapped harmonics (as before).

BEAUTIFUL GIRLS

Words and Music by
Edward Van Halen, Alex Van Halen,
Michael Anthony and David Lee Roth

Tune down ½ step:
⑥ = E♭ ③ = G♭
⑤ = A♭ ② = B♭
④ = D♭ ① = E♭

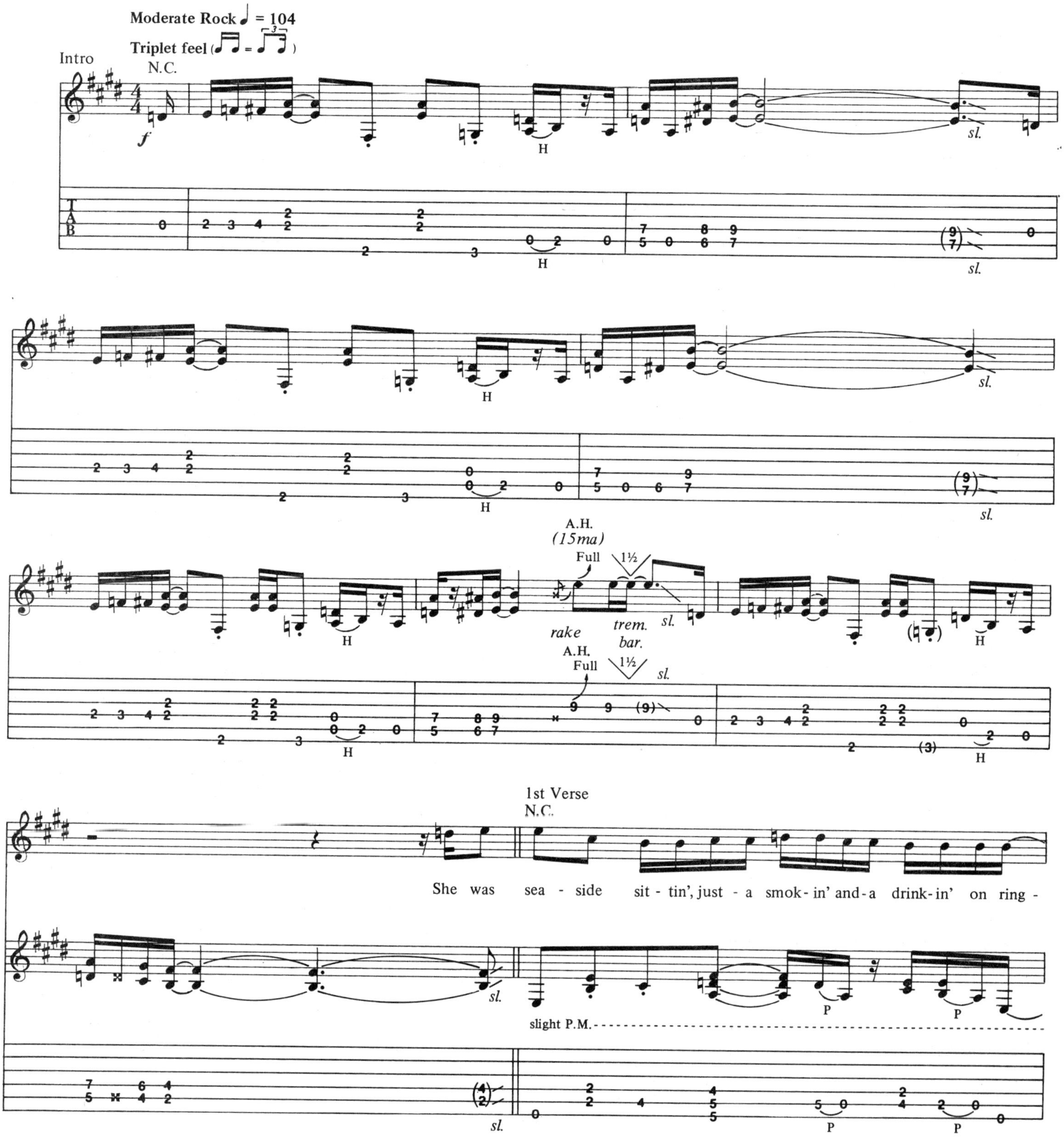

side,___ on top o' the world,__________ oh yeah.___ She had a
P sl. slight P.M. P P P sl.
drink in her hand, she had her toes in the sand, and whoa,___ what a beau - ti - ful
P.M. P.M. slight P.M. P sl.
A5/F#
girl,___________ ah yeah.___ What a
P.M. P.M. P P P.M. sl. sl. P P P.M.
B5
sweet talk - in' hon - ey, with a lit - tle bit o' mon - ey, she turn___ your head a - round.___ Crea - ture
P.M. P.M. P.M. P P P.M. P.M. P.M. P.M. P P

from the sea with the looks to me like she'd like to fool a - round. What a
P.M. P.M. P.M. P.M. P.M.
sl.
N.C.
snap-py lit-tle mam-my, gon-na keep her pap-py hap-py and ac-com-pa-ny me to the ends of the
P.M. P.M.
sl.
Chorus
N.C. E5 F#5 G5
earth, ah yeah. That's what I said. Here I am, ain't no
P.M. P.M.
sl. sl.
N.C. A5 B5 C5 N.C. E5 F#5 G5 N.C. A5 B5 C5
man of the world, no. All I need is a beau-ti - ful girl.
sl. sl. sl.
sl. sl.

G5   C5 D5   N.C.
Ah,   yeah!
(Beau - ti - ful girls.)
(Spoken:) Come here, hon - ey. C' - mon, c' - mon.
Well, I'm a
2nd Verse
N.C.
bum in the sun__ and I'm hav - in' fun,__ and I know you know__ I got no spe - cial plans.__
slight P.M.
(Spe - cial   plans.)__
All the
slight P.M.
trem. bar.
*Depress bar before striking note.
bills are paid, I got it made in the shade and all__ I n-nee - need__ is__ the
slight P.M.

A5/F#
wom - an.
(Un - der - stand?)
What a
slight P.M.
B5
sweet talk-in' hon-ey with a lit-tle bit o' mon-ey, she turn your head a - round. A crea-ture
P.M. P.M. P.M. P.M. P.M. P.M. P.M.
Chorus
N.C. E5 F#5 G5
from the sea with the looks to me like she'd like to fool a - round. Here I am, ain't no
P.M. P.M. P.M. P.M.
N.C. A5 B5 C5
N.C. E5 F#5 G5
N.C. A5 B5 C5
man of the world, no. All I need is a beau-ti-ful girl.
H P sl.
H P sl.
P.M.

G5   C5   D5   B5
Ah,   yeah! Beau-ti-ful girl._______   Oh!_   Come this way, babe.
sl.
P.M.   P.M.   P.M.   P.M.   P.M.
trem. bar. semi-harm.
Guitar solo
A.H. (15ma)
N.C.(F#5)
trem. bar.
A.H.
A.H. pitch: E   sl.
1½ 1½   Full   Full Full   H   P   Full   P   N.C.
sl. sl.
E5   N.C.
Sit-down right here.
H
Ooh_   la   la!_____
Harm. 2½
sl. trem. bar.   H   H
Harm. 2½

(Spoken:) I think I got it now.
Now, I'm-a
sl.
H
P.M.
sl.
3rd Verse
N.C.
sea - side sit - tin', just - a smok - in' and - a drink - in', I'm ring - side, on top o' the world,
P.M.
P
P.M.
uh!
(Top o' the world.)
I got a
P.M.
P
P
slight P.M.
sl. semi-harm.
1/2 1/2
sl.
drink in my hand, I got my toes in the sand, all I need is a beau - ti - ful girl,
Harm. (15ma)
P.M.
P
P.M.
P
sl.
Harm.

uh!
(Beau - ti - ful girl.)
Harm.
(8va)
Oh yeah.
P.M.
Harm.
P
P
P
sl
Chorus
N.C. E5 F#5 G5
N.C. A5 B5 C5
N.C. E5 F#5 G5
Here I am, ain't no man of the world, no. All I need is a
sl.
sl.
sl.
sl.
N.C. A5 B5 C5
G5
C5 D5 E5
N.C.
beau - ti - ful girl.
Ah yeah!
(Beau - ti - ful girls.)
(Spoken:) I ain't lyin' to
rake reverse rake
sl.
P.M.
sl.
D5
A5
E5
D5
Voc. Fig. 1
ya.
Nothin' else I need.
Ah yeah! Beau - ti - ful girls.
Set yourself on down.
Ah
sl. sl.
P P
P P
P.M. P.M.
P P
P P
P.M.
P P

w/Voc. Fig. 1 (9 times)
A5
N.C.(E5)
D5
trem. pick.
sl.
A5
N.C.(E5)
D5
A5
N.C.(E5)
D5
(Spoken:) C'm here, baby. C'm here.
trem. bar
A5
N.C.(E5)
D5
What's your name, honey? What's your... Hey, hey, where you goin'?
trem. bar
A5
N.C.(E5)
D5
A5
N.C.(E5)
Hey!
Hey!
trem. bar.
Hey, babe, wait...

6
3
sl.
sl.
sl.
D5
A5
N.C.(E5)
sl.
sl.
I love 'em! I need 'em!
sl. sl.
sl. sl. sl. sl.
sl.
D5
A5
N.C.(E5)
D5
Can't do with-out 'em! No!
P.M.
P P sl. sl. sl. P H P sl. P
sl.
A5
N.C.(E5)
D5
Ah
trem.
bar.
sl.
sl.
*w/Voc. Fig. 1
A5
E5
**
yeah! Beau-ti-ful girls.
P P
sl. sl.
echo
*Substitute half rest for last 2 beats.
P P
sl.
**Kissing sound.

AND THE CRADLE WILL ROCK...

Words and Music by
Edward Van Halen, David Lee Roth,
Alex Van Halen and Michael Anthony

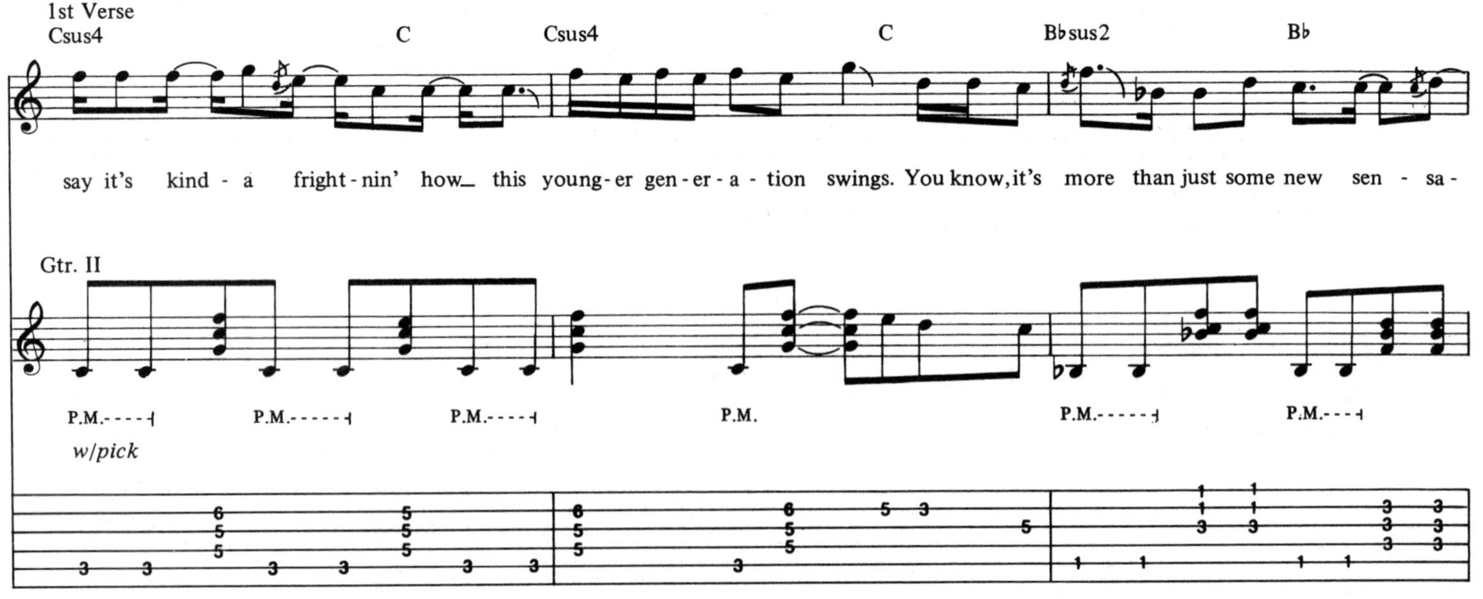
A5   C5/A   G5/A   A5   C5/A   D5/G
Ow!   Ow!   Well, they
(Gtr. III out)
trem.
pick
trem. pick
(end Rhy. Fig. 1)
1st Verse
Csus4   C   Csus4   C   Bbsus2   Bb
say it's kind-a fright-nin' how_ this young-er gen-er-a-tion swings. You know, it's more than just some new sen-sa-
Gtr. II
P.M.   P.M.   P.M.   P.M.   P.M.   P.M.
w/pick

Csus4
C
Csus4
C
tion. Well, the kid is in - to los - in' sleep, and he don't come home for half the week. You know, it's
Gtr. III
Fdbk.
(8va)
Fdbk.
sl.
sl.
sl.
Fdbk. pitch: E♭
sl.
sl.
sl.
(Gtr. II)
P
P
P.M. P.M. P.M. P.M. P.M. P.M. P.M.
Bb
w/Fill 1
N.C.
Chorus
w/Rhy. Fig. 1 (1st 7 bars only)
A5
C5/A
G5/A
more than just an ag - gra - va - tion. And the cra - dle will rock.
Riff A
pick slide
trem. pick
(cont. in
Rhy. Fig. I)
P.M. P.M.
w/fingers

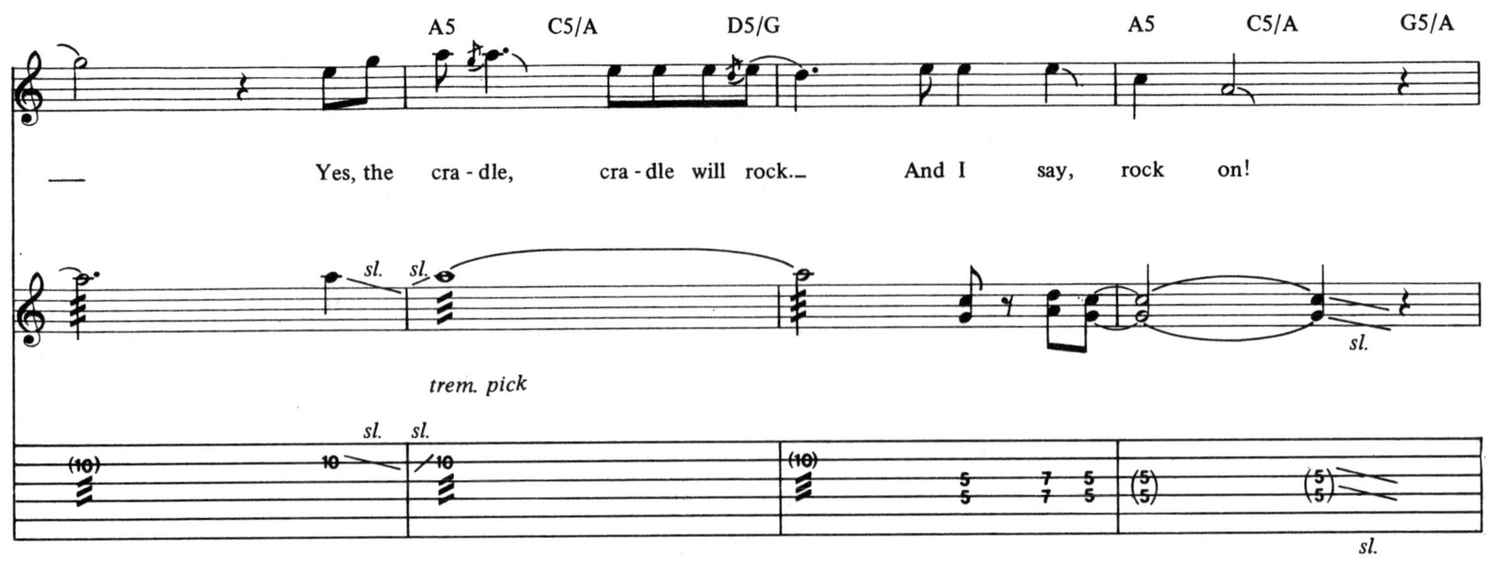

A5   C5/A   D5/G   A5   C5/A   G5/A
Yes, the cra - dle, cra - dle will rock.__ And I say, rock on!
trem. pick
sl. sl.
sl.
(10) 10 10 (10) 5 7 5 (5) (5)
5 7 5 5 5
sl.

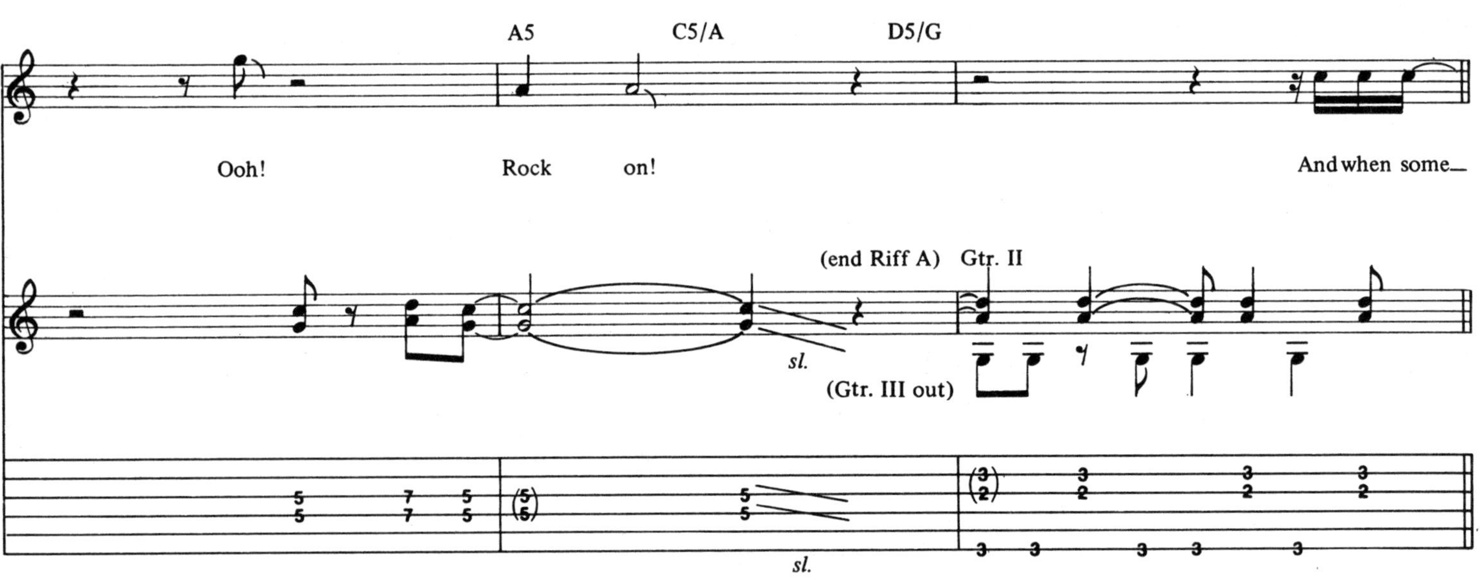

A5   C5/A   D5/G
Ooh!   Rock   on!   And when some__
(end Riff A) Gtr. II
(Gtr. III out)
sl.
5 7 5 (5) 5 (3) 3 3 3
5 7 5 5 5 2 2 2 2
sl. 3 3 3 3 3

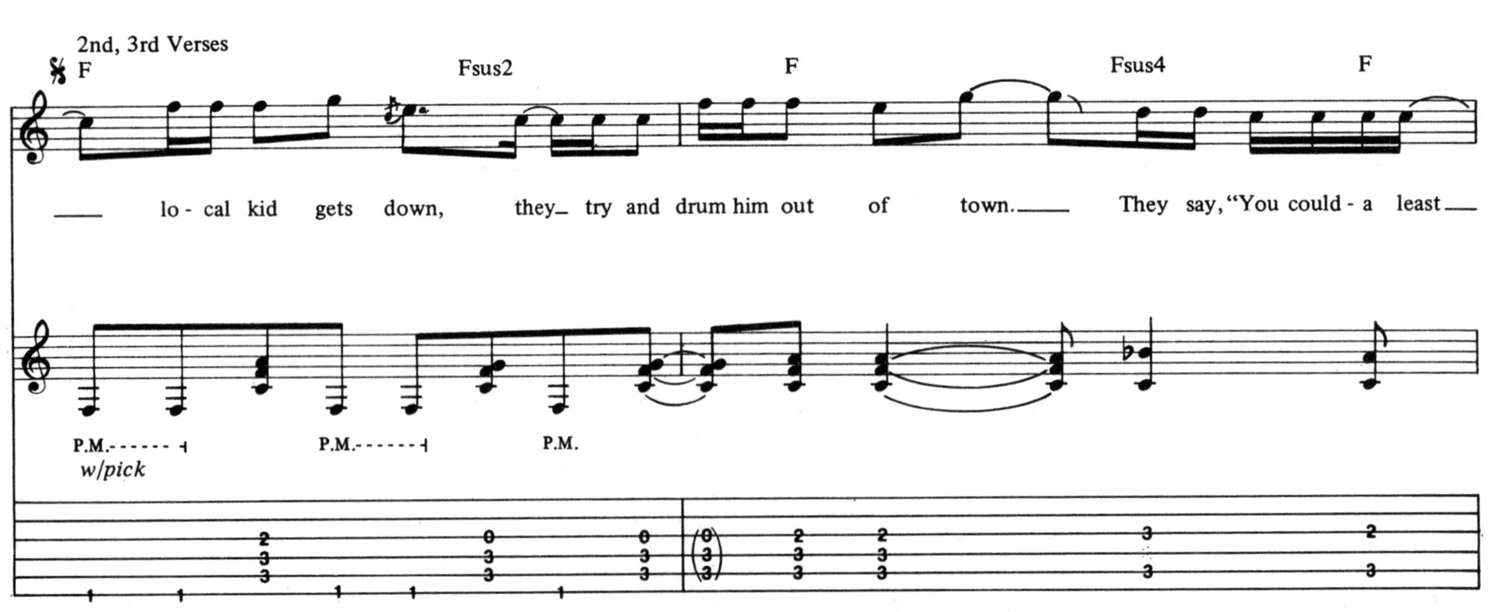

2nd, 3rd Verses
F   Fsus2   F   Fsus4   F
__ lo - cal kid gets down, they__ try and drum him out of town.__ They say, "You could - a least __
P.M. P.M. P.M.
w/pick
2 0 0 (0) 2 2 3 2
2 0 3 (3) 3 3 3
3 3 3 3 3 3
1 1 1 1 1 1

1st time w/Fill 2
Eb   Ebsus#4   Eb5   F   Fsus2
faked it, boy, faked it, boy."
1. At an ear-ly age he hits the street and winds
2. And so an
P.M.   P.M.----   P.M.
P.M.----   P.M.----   P.M.

F   Fsus4   F   Eb   Ebsus#4   Eb5   w/Fill 1   N.C.
up tied with who he meets, and he's
1. un-em - ployed, un-em - ployed. Ow!
2. un-em - ployed. His folks are o - ver - joyed.
And the
w/fingers

Chorus
w/Rhy. Fig. 1 (1st 7 bars only) and Riff A
A5   C5/A   G5/A   2nd time Gtr. III subst. Fill 4   A5   C5/A   D5/G
cra - dle will rock.
1. Ow! And the cra - dle, the cra - dle will rock.
2. Yes, the cra - dle, cra - dle will rock.
To Coda

1st time Gtr. II subst. Rhy. Fill 1   A5   C5/A   G5/A   A5   C5/A   D5/G
And I say, rock on!
I say, rock on!
Oh!   Rock on!
Hey!

Fill 2
Gtr. III
Full Full Full Full Full

Rhy. Fill 1
Gtr. II
P   P
P   P

Fill 4
Gtr. III
H P
H P

Guitar solo
Gtr. IV
C
Bb
C/Bb
Full
Full
grad. release
Gtr. II
(w/fingers)
F/A
Fm/Ab
Gsus4
G
Gsus4
G Fsus2
rake
Full
C
Cm
8va-
w/Fill 1
N.C.
rit.
(Spoken:) Have you seen junior's grades? (Sob.)
rit.
(cont. in Rhy. Fig. 1)

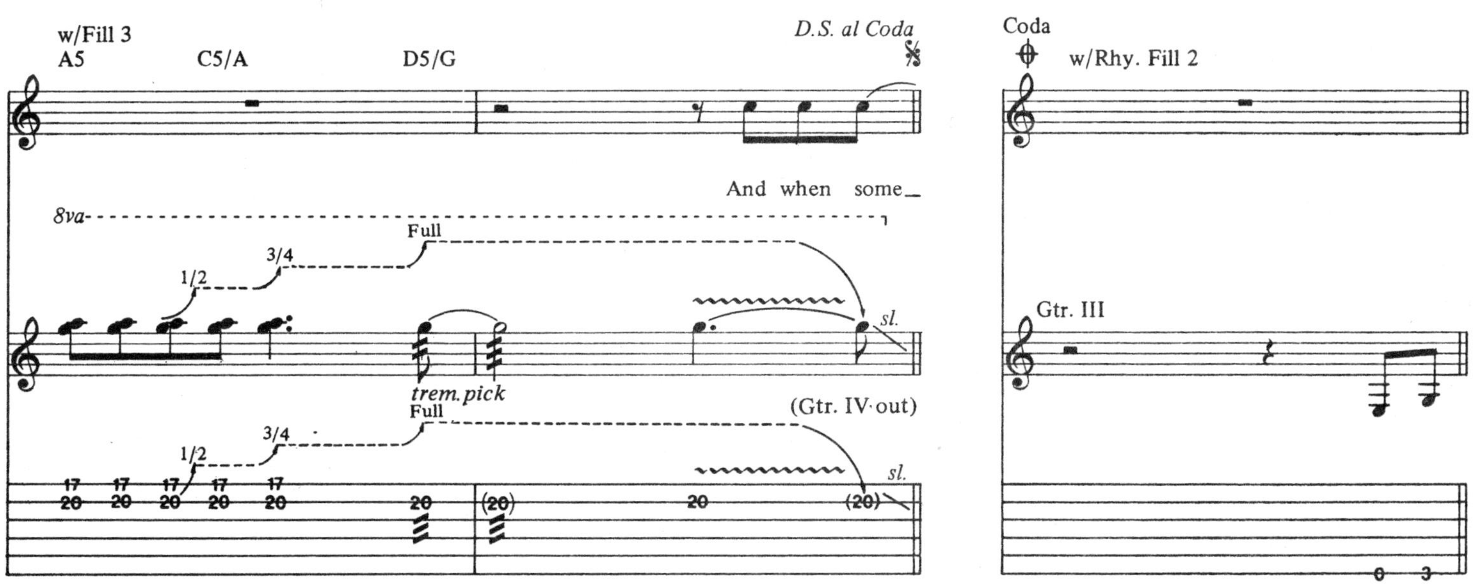

w/Rhy. Fig. 1
A5   C5/A   G5/A   A5   C5/A   D5/G
Gtr. IV
Full
Full   Full   sl.   sl.   sl.
A5   C5/A   G5/A
Full   Full   Full   P H T P   T P H T P   T P H T P   sl.
w/Fill 3
A5   C5/A   D5/G   D.S. al Coda   Coda   w/Rhy. Fill 2
And when some
8va
1/2   3/4   Full
trem. pick   (Gtr. IV out)
Gtr. III

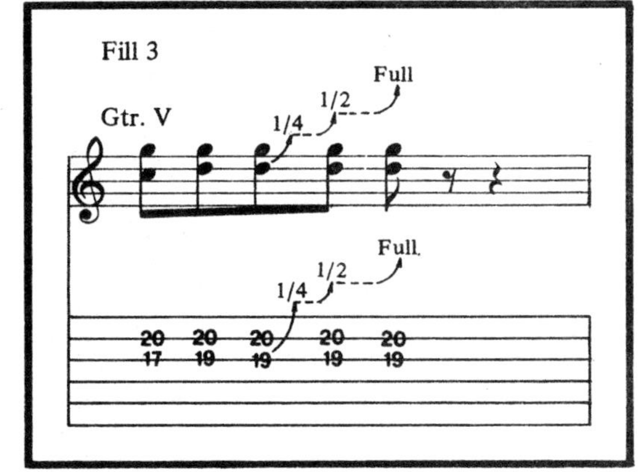

Fill 3
Full
Gtr. V
1/4   1/2
1/4   1/2   Full

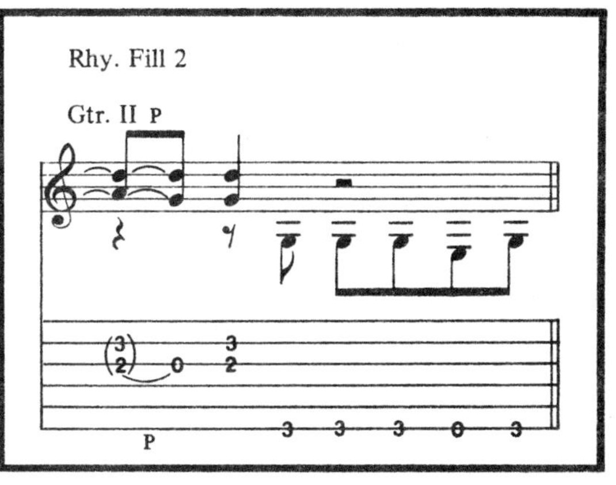

Rhy. Fill 2
Gtr. II P
P

Outro
w/Rhy. Fig. 1(1st 4 bars only)
w/vocal ad lib (till end)
A5   C5/A   G5/A   A5   C5/A   D5/G
Rock on!
Rock on!
8va-
1/4   1/2   Full
sl.
Gtr. IV
Full
trem. pick
Play 2nd time only
Full
1/4   1/2   Full
sl.
trem. pick
Gtr. III
sl.
sl.
w/Rhy. Fig. 1 (1st 4 bars only)
A5   C5/A   G5/A   A5   C5/A   D5/G
Repeat and fade
Rock on!
Rock on!
8va-
Full
trem. pick
Full
P.M.-   P.M.
P.M.-   P.M.
sl.
sl.
sl.

EVERYBODY WANTS SOME!!

Words and Music by
Edward Van Halen, David Lee Roth,
Alex Van Halen and Michael Anthony

Tune down 1/2 step:
⑥ = E♭ ③ = G♭
⑤ = A♭ ② = B♭
④ = D♭ ① = E♭

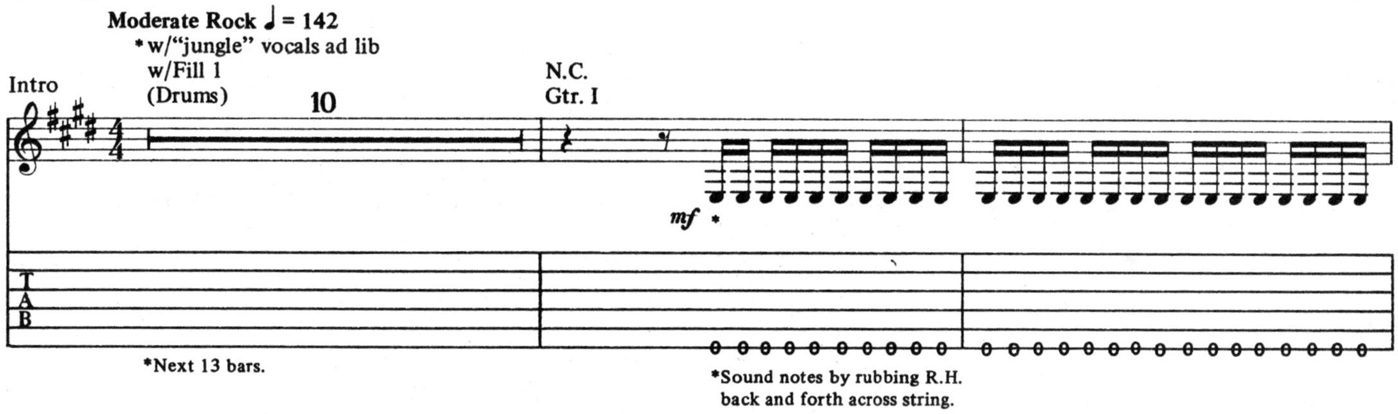

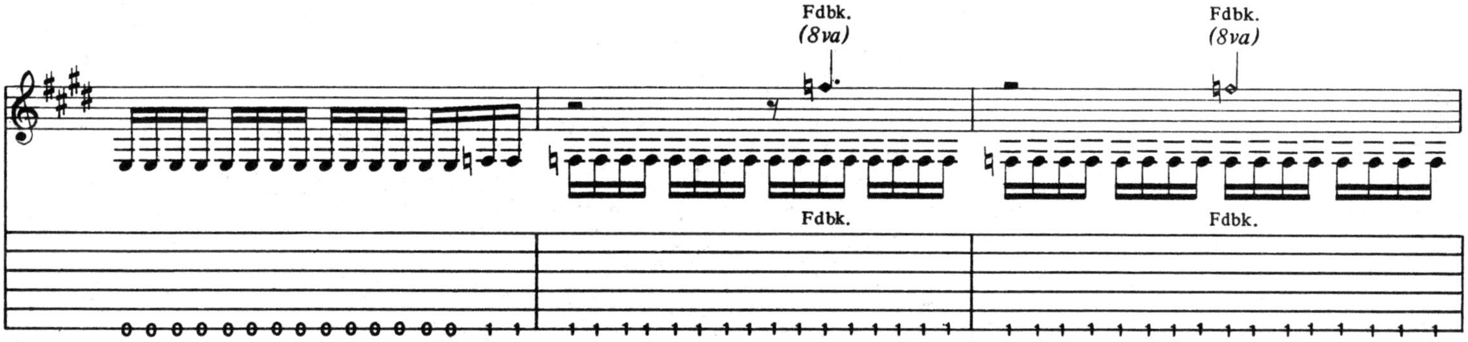

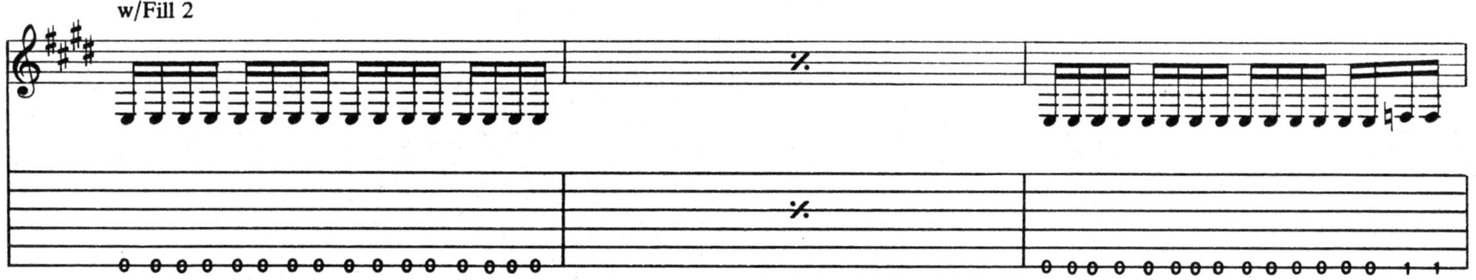

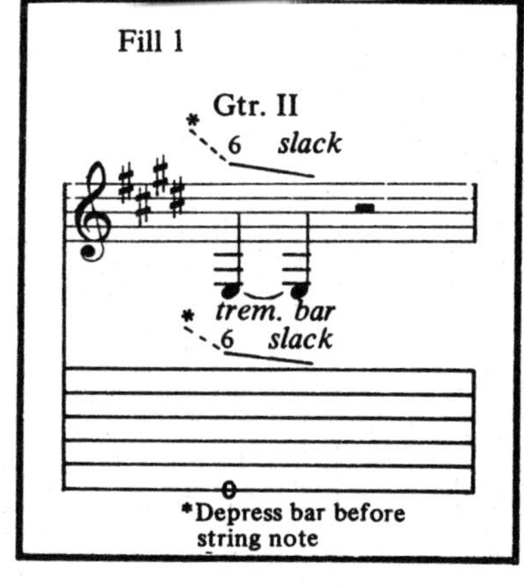

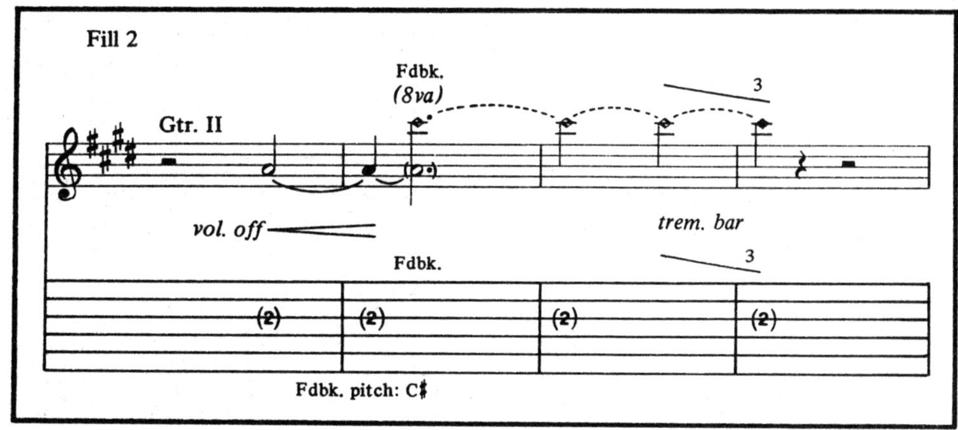

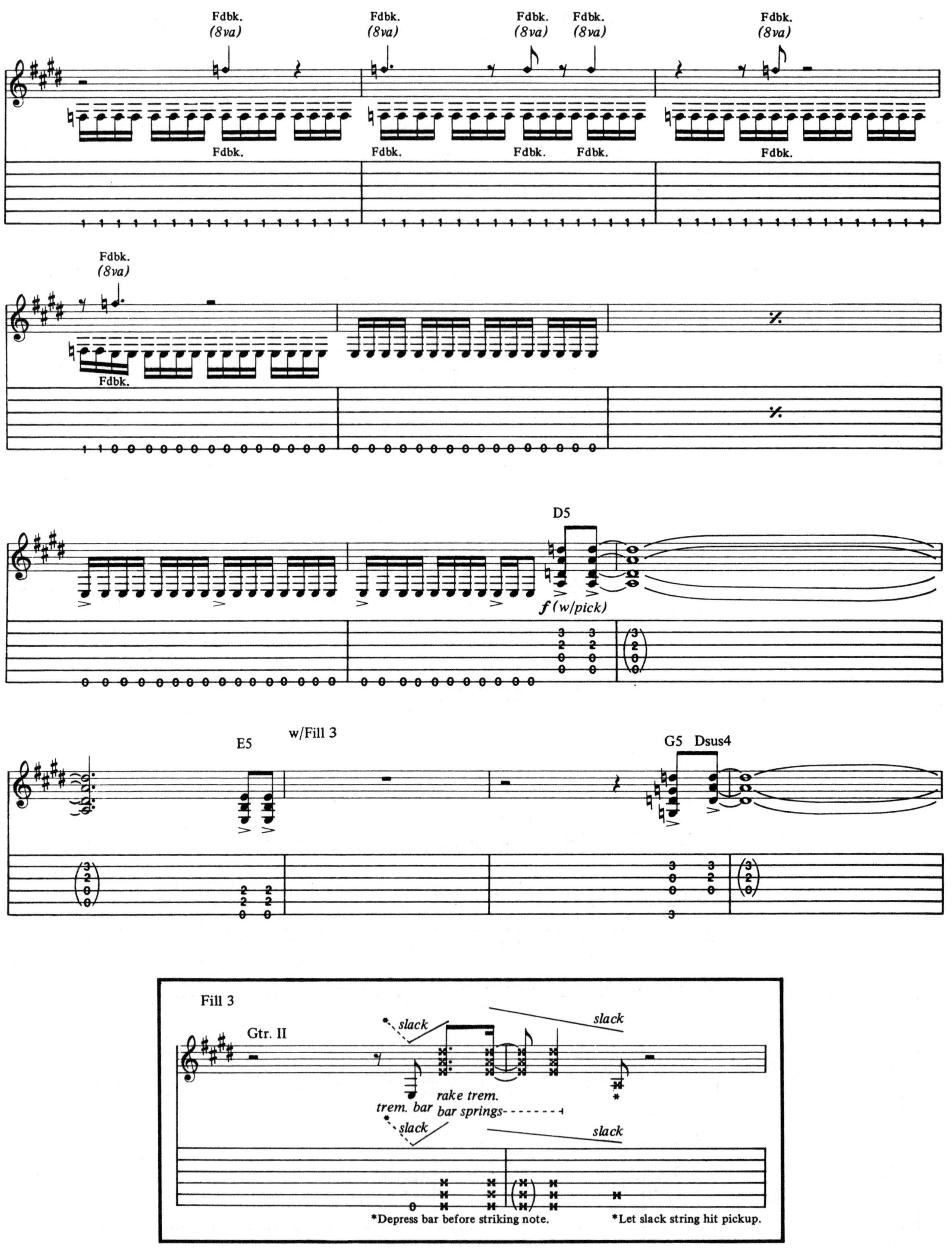

Fdbk.
(8va)
Fdbk.
D5
E5
w/Fill 3
G5 Dsus4
f (w/pick)
Fill 3
Gtr. II
slack
slack
rake trem.
trem. bar   bar springs
slack
slack
*Depress bar before striking note.
*Let slack string hit pickup.

w/Fill 4
E5
Dsus4
let ring
sl.
let ring
sl.
w/Fill 5
E5
D5
trem. bar
w/Fill 6
E5
Dsus4
trem. bar
P.M.
Fill 4
Gtr. II
pick scrapes
*Push string into
pickup.
Fill 5
A.H.
(15ma)
Gtr. II
rake
trem. bar (slow dive)
A.H.
A.H. pitch: C#
Fill 6
Gtr. II
pick scrapes

D
Ow!
E5   A5   D5   E5   A5
Oh yeah!
1/2
P.M.   P.M.   1/2
D5   E5   A5   D5
Oh yeah!
1/2   1/2
P.M.   P.M.   1/2
E5   A5   D5   E5   1st Verse
You can't   get ro - man - tic on a
P.M.   P.M.
sl. P tram. bar
sl. P

D5 E5
sub - way line.
slack
Full
trem. bar
1½
H
Full
1½
(7) 8 7
(8 7)
7 9
7 9
5 7
(0)
duc - tor don't like it, says you're wast-in' your time.
A.H. (15ma)
Full
sl.
grad. bend
A.H.
Full
(9 9 7) (9 9 7)
sl.
*Rub R.H. back and forth across stg.
0 6 (6)
0 0 0 0
Chorus
E5
A5
D5
But ev - 'ry - bod - y wants some.
I want some
1/2
trem. bar
P.M.
P.M.
(0 6)
3 4
2 0
(2 0)
0
2 0
(2 0)
0
1/2
3
3 2 0
4 2
E5
A5
D5
E5
A5
too.
Ev - 'ry - bod - y wants some.
P.M.
P.M.
1/2
1/2
P.M.
P.M.
2 0
2 0
0
(0)
3
3 2 0
4 2
2 0
2 0
2 0

D5
E5
A5
D5
E5
Ba - by, how 'bout you? Oh, yeah, yeah!
P.M.
P.M.
1/2
2nd Verse
I've seen the peo - ple that are look - in' for a moon - beam.
slack
trem. bar
slack
H
3/4
trem. bar
D5 E5
Oh! Oh yeah, ya spent a lot. Ya got lost in the jet stream.
sl.
sl.
semi-harm.
Chorus
E5
A5
Ooh, ev - 'ry - bod - y wants some.
trem. bar
1/2
3½
P

D5
E5
A5
D5
I want some too. Oh yeah. Ev - 'ry - bod - y
1/2
1/2
P.M.
P.M.
1/2
1/2

E5
A5
D5
E5
A5
wants some. How 'bout you? Oh
P.M. P.M.
1/2
1/2
P.M.
P.M.

D5
E5
D/F#
yeah! Ooh,
1/2
P.M. P.M. P.M. P.M.
1/2

G
A5
E5
D/F#
yeah, yeah, yeah, yeah, yeah, yeah, yeah.
P.M. P.M. P.M. P.M. P.M. P.M.

N.C.
P.M.
Guitar solo
D5
Gtr. II
trem. bar
semi-harm.
Gtr. I
P.M.
E5
sl.
D5

E5
D5
E5
D5
H P P H Full Full
trem. pick
P.M.
sl.
8va
59

Chorus
E5 E5 A5 D5 E5 A5
Ev-'ry-bod-y wants some.___ I want some too.___ Woh.___
(Gtr. II out)
1/2 Full 1½
grad. bend
1/2 Full 1½
sl.
P.M.
D5 E5 A5 D5
Ev-'ry-bod-y wants some. Hey, hey!___ How 'bout___ you?___
1/2
P.M. P.M.
E5 A5 D5 E5
Oh yeah!___
P.M. P.M.
sl. trem. bar

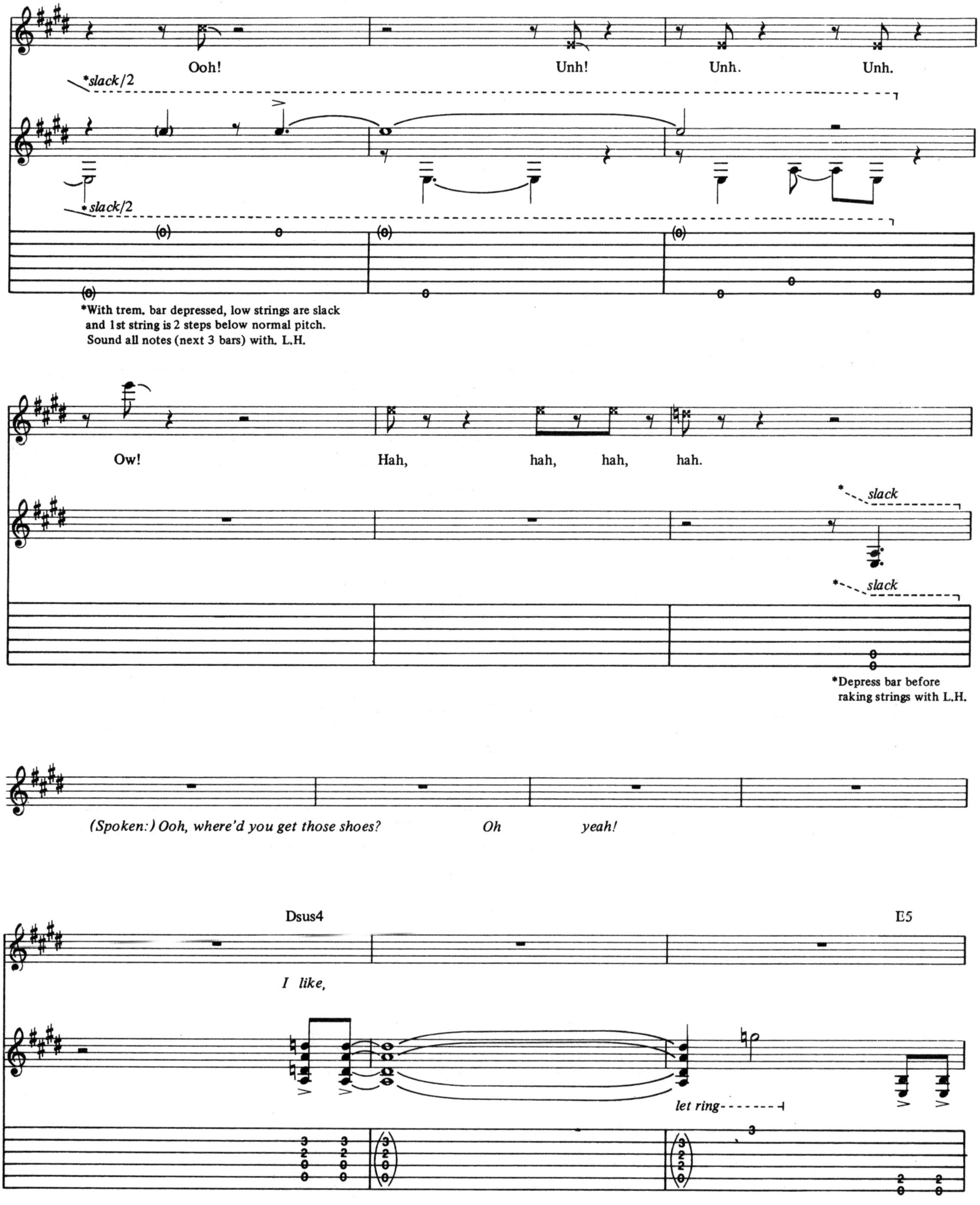

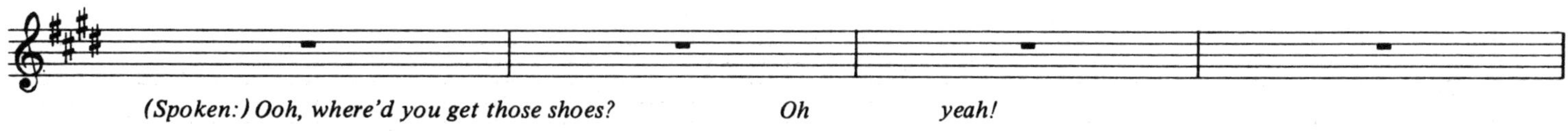

Ooh!   Unh!   Unh.   Unh.

*slack/2

*slack/2

(o)   o   (o)   (o)

*With trem. bar depressed, low strings are slack
and 1st string is 2 steps below normal pitch.
Sound all notes (next 3 bars) with. L.H.

Ow!   Hah,   hah,   hah,   hah.

*   slack

*   slack

*Depress bar before
raking strings with L.H.

(Spoken:) Ooh, where'd you get those shoes?   Oh   yeah!

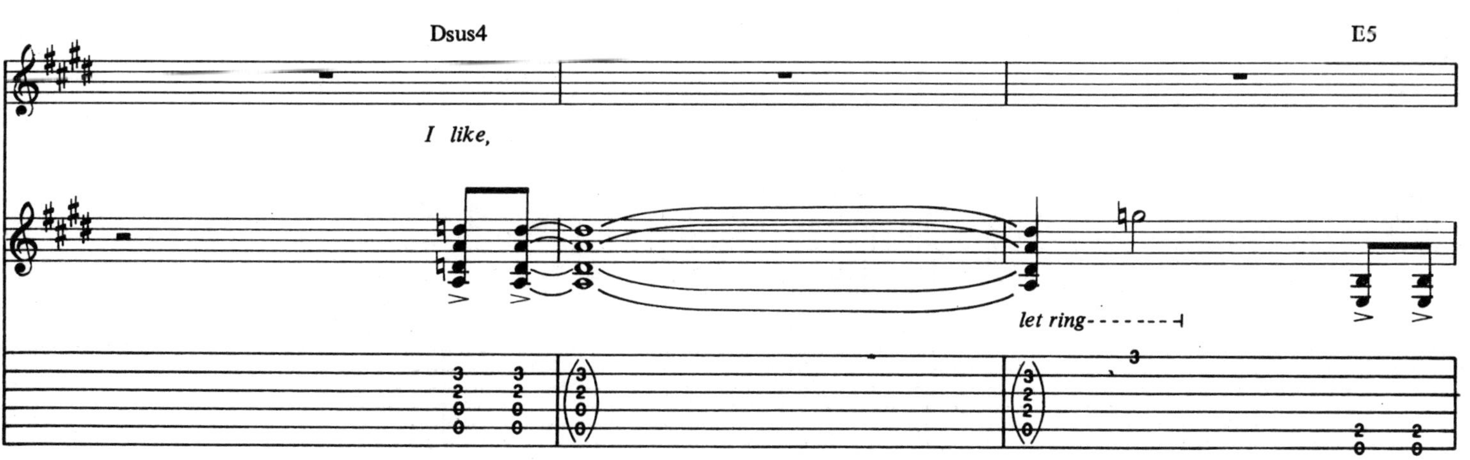

Dsus4   E5

I like,

let ring

3

Dsus4
I like the way the line runs up the back of the stockings.
E5
Dsus4
I've always like those kind of high heels too. You know, I...
trem. bar
1½
1½
6
6 trem. bar
E5
No, no, no, no, don't take 'em off, don't take...
trem. bar
1½
1½
Dsus4
E5
Leave 'em on, leave 'em on.
trem. bar
4½
4½

D5

Yeah, that's it, a little more to the right, a little more...

Ow! _______

H - h - hey, hey, hey!

Ev - 'ry - bod - y

Chorus
E5   A5   D5   E5   A5

wants   some.   I   want   some   too. _______   Woh. _______

D5   E5   A5   D5

______ Ev - 'ry - bod - y wants   some.   Ba - by, how 'bout   you? _______

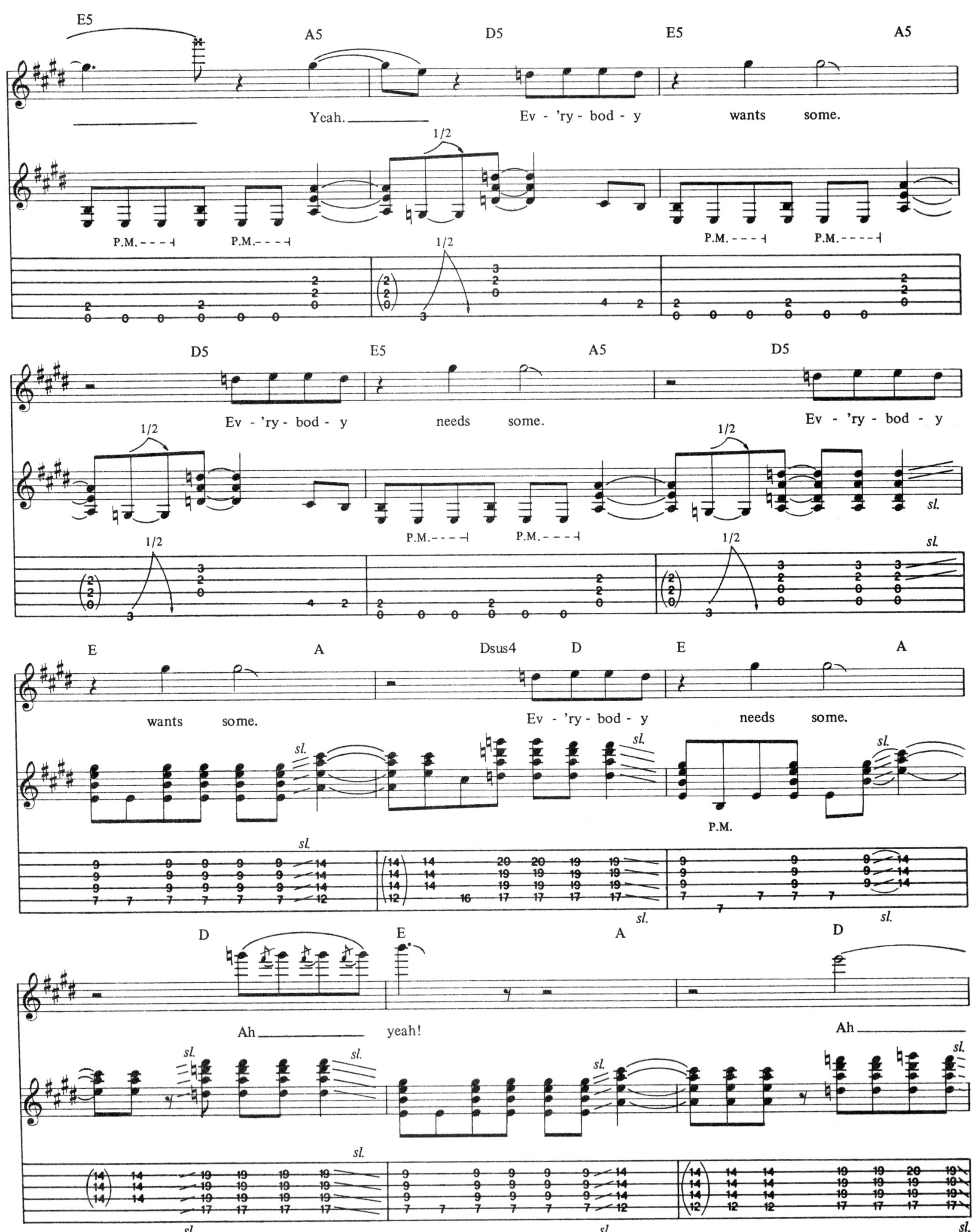

E5
A5
D5
E5
A5
Yeah. Ev-'ry-bod-y wants some.
P.M. P.M.
1/2
1/2
D5
E5
A5
D5
Ev-'ry-bod-y needs some.
1/2
P.M. P.M.
1/2
sl.
sl.
E
A
Dsus4
D
E
A
wants some. Ev-'ry-bod-y needs some.
sl.
sl.
sl.
P.M.
sl.
sl.
D
E
A
D
Ah yeah! Ah
sl.
sl.
sl.
sl.
sl.

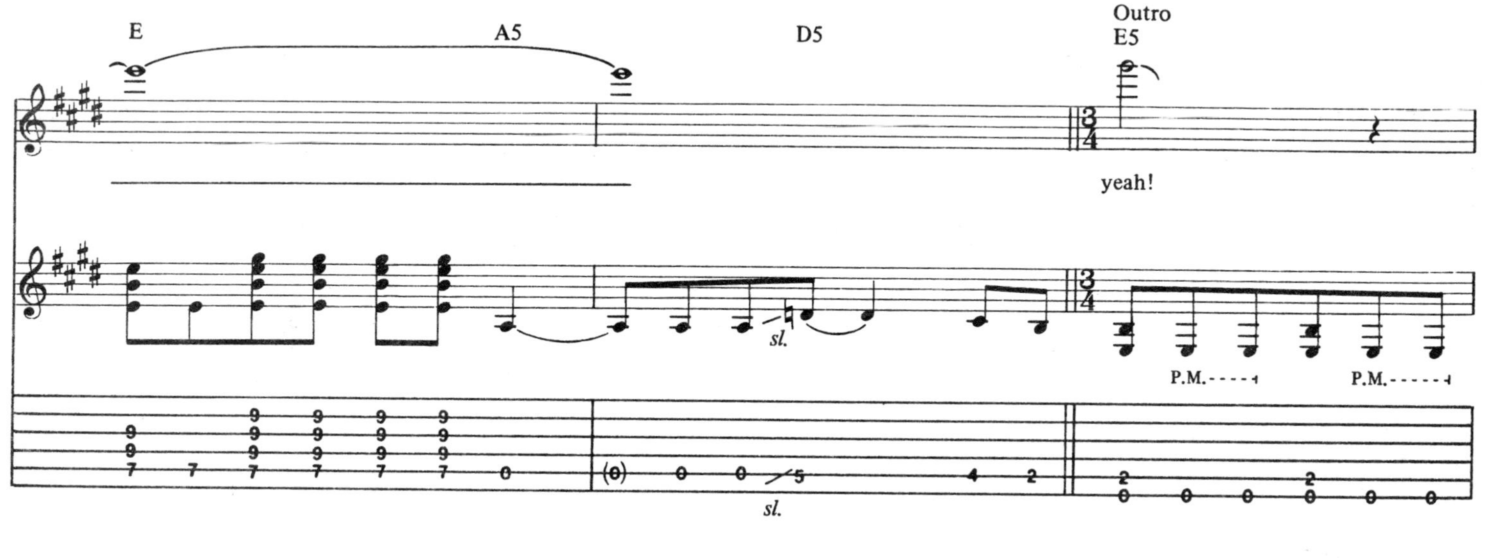

E
A5
D5
Outro
E5
yeah!
P.M.
P.M.
sl.
sl.

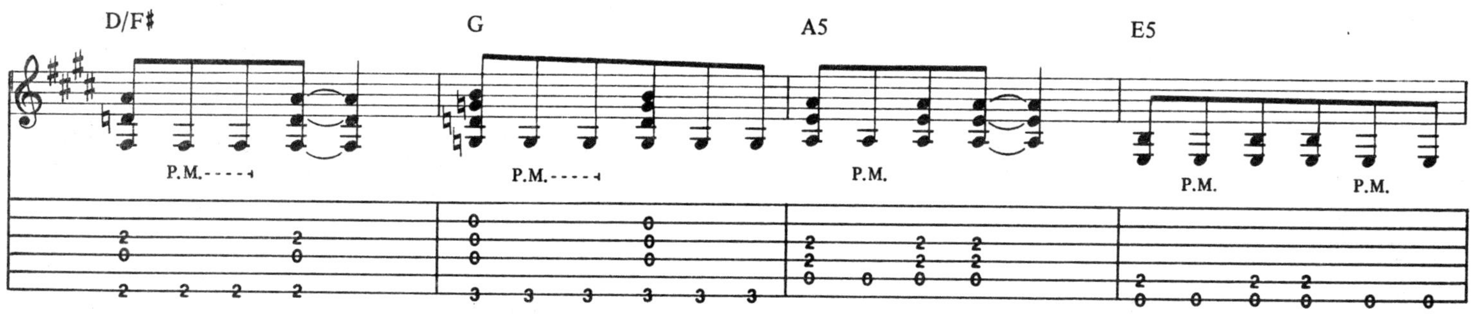

D/F#
G
A5
E5
P.M.
P.M.
P.M.
P.M.
P.M.

D/F#
G
A
P.M.
P.M.
rit.

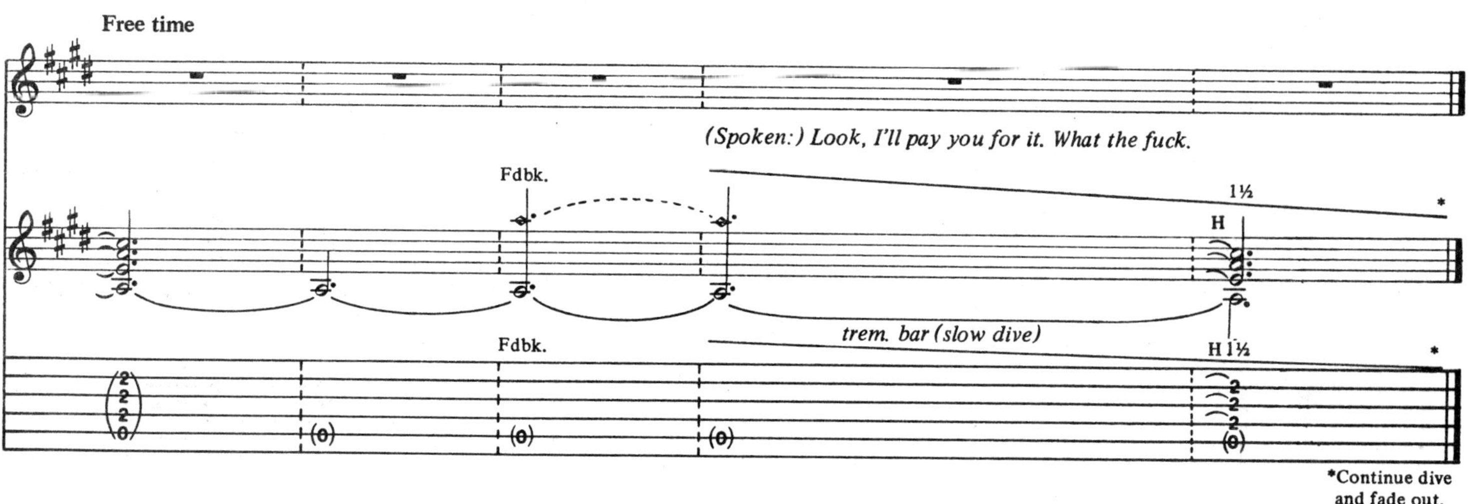

Free time
(Spoken:) Look, I'll pay you for it. What the fuck.
Fdbk.
Fdbk.
1½
H
trem. bar (slow dive)
H 1½
*
*
*Continue dive
and fade out.

TAKE YOUR WHISKEY HOME

Words and Music by
Edward Van Halen, David Lee Roth,
Alex Van Halen and Michael Anthony

But I like that bot-tle bet-ter than the rest. And she said: I

Chorus
Gm7
think that you're head-ed for a whole lot of trou-ble, ah! Well, I

think that you're head-ed for a whole lot of trou-ble. Well, I

think that you're head-ed for a whole lot of trou-ble. If you take your whis-key...

G5
(Gtr. I out)
Gtr. II (elec.)

(Band in)
Gm7
pick slide
sl.
*pick slide
steady gliss.
P.M.
H
*Tap edge of pick onto fretboard and slide past end of fretboard.
sl.
H
P.M.
pick slide
sl.
P.M.
H P H P H P H P
sl.
H P H P H P H P
sl.
G
2nd Verse
Gm7
Well, that liq - uor in the night - time leaves strange mem - o - ries. Seems a life-
A.H. (15ma)
sl.
steady gliss.
P.M.
P.M.
P.M.
P.M.
A.H.
A.H. pitch: B
time, ooh, since yes - ter - day. Come the day - break and come to - mor-
A.H. (15ma)
A.H. (15ma)
H P
P.M.
P.M.
P.M.
P.M.
A.H.
A.H.
H P
A.H. pitch: D
A.H. pitch: B

row,_____ that wom-an's wait-ed up__ all night for__ me a-gain.__ Oh! She said: Well, I

P.M.---- P.M.----------- P.M.----- P.M.----------- P.M.---- P.M.----------

Chorus
Am7
think that you're head-ed for a whole lot of trou-ble,________ yeah.____________ I

P.M.------- P.M.----------------- P.M.-------- P.M.----------- H P

think that you're head-ed for a whole lot of trou-ble. Ooh yeah.___ Yeah, you_

A.H.
(15ma)

P.M. P.M.------------ P.M.------- A.H. P.M.-----------------

__ know that you're head-ed for a lot of trou-ble if you

P.M.----------------- P.M.------- P.M.-----------------

A5
take your whis - key home.
A.H.
(15ma)
P.M.
A.H.
P.M.
Guitar solo I
*B5
Full
1/2
Full
1/2
Full
A.H.
(15ma)
1/2
1½
H
rake
Full
1/2
Full
1/2
P
Full
A.H.
1/2
1½
H
*Chord name derived
from bass gtr.
A.H. pitch: A#
Some goes to wom -
P
H H
P H
sl.
P P H P P H P P
H
sl. sl.
P
1½
2
H
sl.
3
6
3
3
rake
grad.
bend
1½
2
pick
slide
P
H H
P H
sl.
P P H P P H P P
P H
sl. sl.
P
15
*Reach over with L.H.
to fret B (3 4fr.).
H
sl.
3rd Verse
Gm7
en, ooh, — some goes — to Je - sus, though I'm ab - so - lute - ly cer - tain both's all right. —
A.H.
(15ma)
P.M.
P.M.
P.M.
semi-
harm.
P.M.
P.M.
A.H.
P.M.

Oh, but it takes__ me__ at least half-way to the la - bel____ 'fore__
A.H. (15ma)
A.H. (15ma)
P.M. rake
semi-harm.
P P P
P.M.
P.M.
P.M.
A.H.
P
A.H.
A.H. pitch: F
P P
A.H. pitch: D

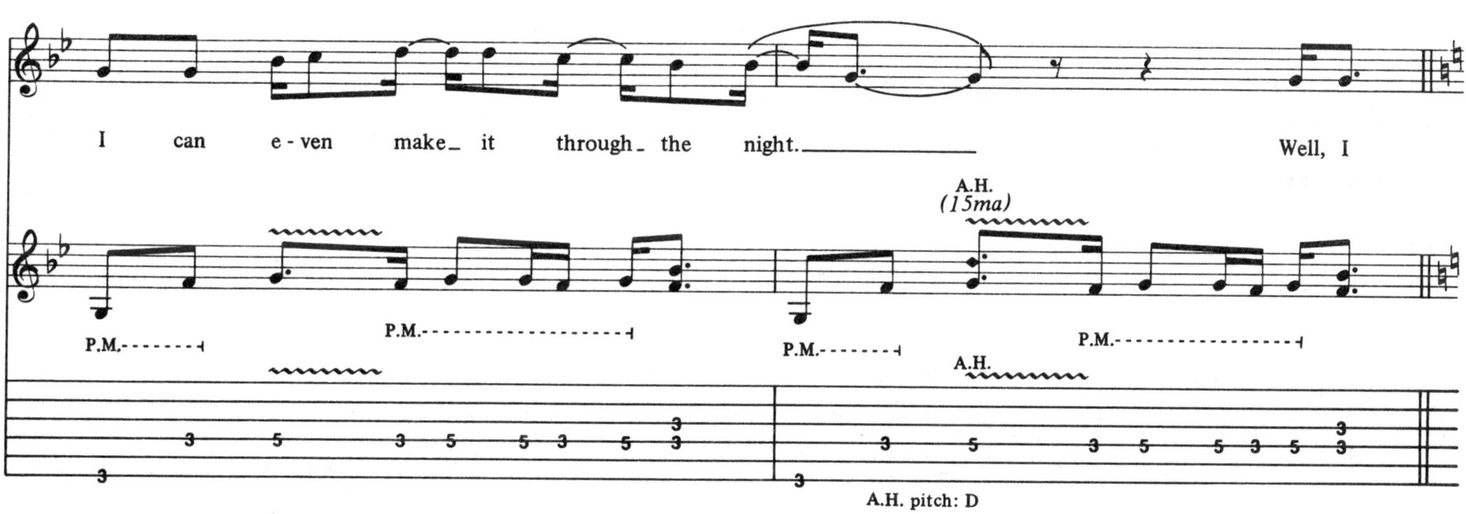

I can e - ven make__ it through__ the night.____ Well, I
A.H. (15ma)
P.M.
P.M.
P.M.
P.M.
A.H.
A.H. pitch: D

Chorus
Am7
think that you're head - ed for a whole lot of trou - ble,____ yeah.____ I
P.M.
P.M.
P.M.
P.M.
H P
H P

think that you're head-ed for a whole lot of trou-ble.___ Ba - by, yes, I ___ think that ___ you're head-ed for ___ some
trou - ble   if you   take   your   whis - key   home.
Guitar solo II
*B5
*Chord names derived from bass gtr. (next 8 bars).

8va-
w/delay
P P H H P P H H P P H H P P H P P
P
rake
grad. bend
5
3
2
3
6
1½
1½
8va-
2 sl. sl.
grad.
bend
2
Full
sl.
loco
H
H
Full
P
Full
P
Full Full
sl.
2
6
6
3
3
(delay off)
H
Outro
Dm7
Ah!
Ooh, ba-by, take your whis-key home.
Yeah.
La la la la la
pick
slide
sl.
steady gliss.
steady gliss.
sl.
P.M.
sl.
la la.
pick
slide
sl.
steady gliss.
trem. bar
1/2
1/2
sl.
D5
sl.

MEAN STREET

Words and Music by
Edward Van Halen, David Lee Roth,
Alex Van Halen and Michael Anthony

Tune down 1/2 step:
⑥ =Eb ③ =Gb
⑤ =Ab ② =Bb
④ =Db ① =Eb
Moderate Rock ♩ = 132
N.C.
Intro
*Ti l.h. Tp l.h.
pp (Fade in)
cresc.
mf
*Ti =Tap both notes w/r.h. index fin.;
l.h. =Slap & mute low stgs. w/left hand;
Tp =Tap w/r.h. thumb.
A.H.
Harm.
(8va)
Free time
Fdbk.
(15ma)
trem. bar
Fdbk. pitches D# D D# B C B A E F
sounded: *Depress bar before sounding Fdbk.

Slower ♩ = 100
N.C.(Am)
G
N.C.(Am)
Harm.
(8va)
P.M.
sim.
P.M.
P.M.
P.M.
Harm.
H P
H P

C5
At night I
H P
P.M.
P.M.
P.M.
w/flanger
H P

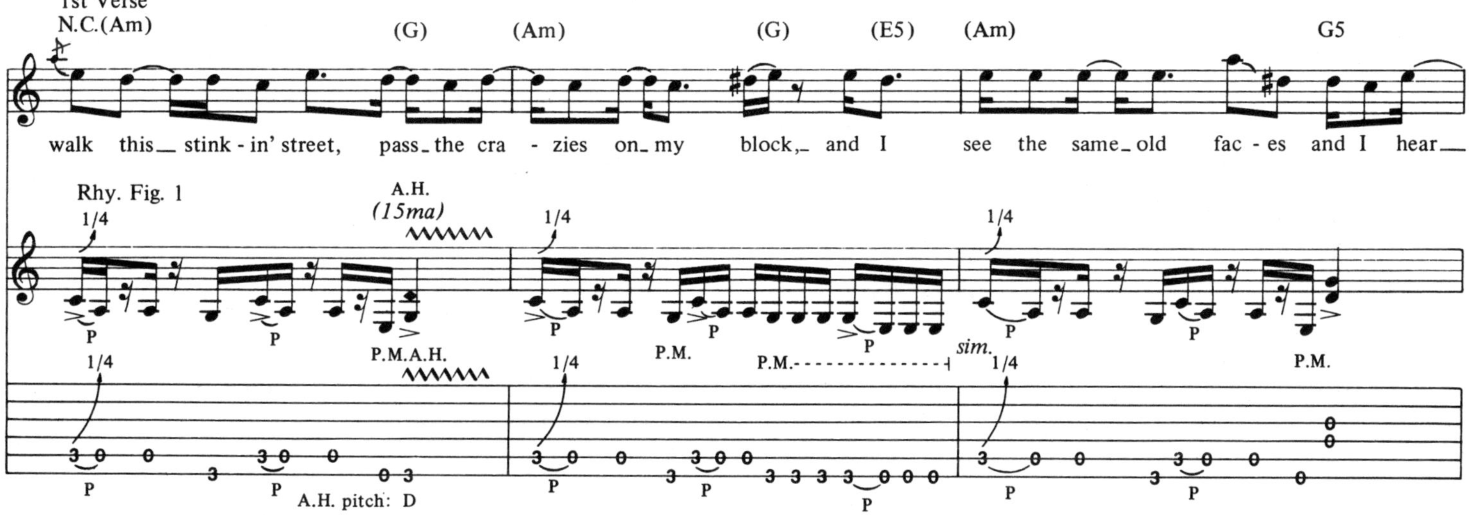

1st Verse
N.C.(Am)
(G)
(Am)
(G)
(E5)
(Am)
G5
walk this stink-in' street, pass the cra - zies on my block, and I see the same old fac - es and I hear
Rhy. Fig. 1
A.H.
(15ma)
1/4
1/4
1/4
1/4
P
P
P
P
P.M.A.H.
P.M.
P.M.
sim.
P.M.
A.H. pitch: D

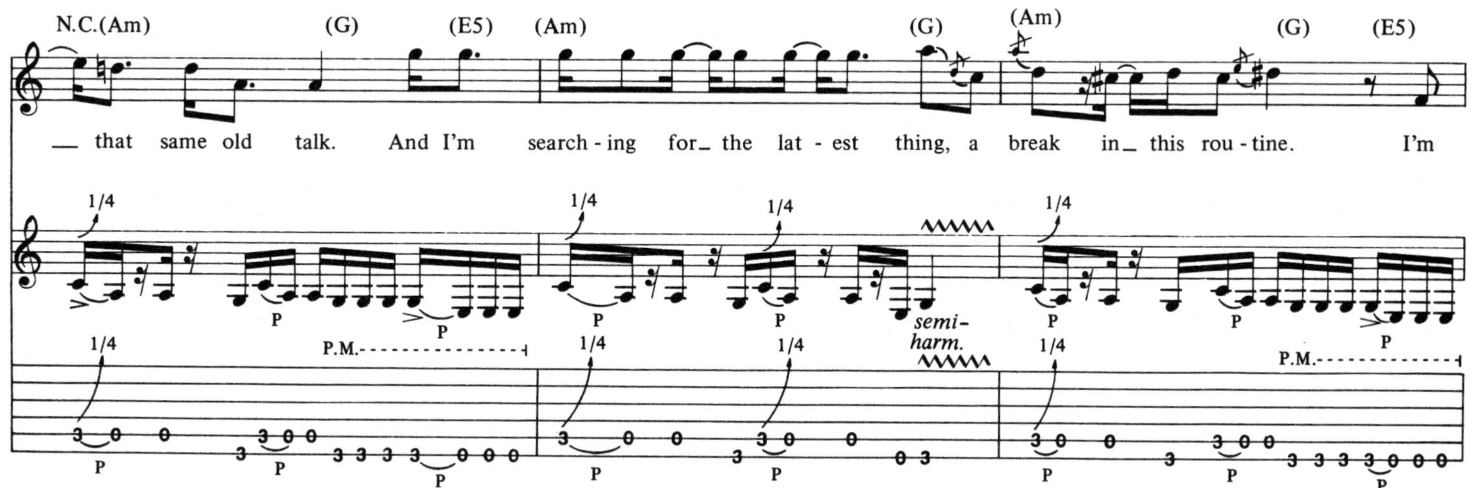

N.C.(Am)
(G)
(E5)
(Am)
(G)
(Am)
(G)
(E5)
that same old talk. And I'm search-ing for the lat - est thing, a break in this rou - tine. I'm
1/4
1/4
1/4
1/4
P
P
P
semi-
harm.
P
P
1/4
P.M.
1/4
1/4
P.M.
P
P
P
P
P

(Am)   (G)   (Am)   (G)   (E5)
talk - in' some new kicks, ones like - a you ain't nev - er seen._ This is
1/4   1/4   1/4   (end Rhy. Fig. 1)
semi-harm.
P.M.
Chorus
N.C.(A5)   Am7   N.C.(A5)   D5/A   N.C.(A5)   F5/A   F5   G5
home,   this is Mean Street.
1/4   A.H. (15ma)   1/4   A.H. (15ma)   1/4
P.M.   sl.   P.M.   P.M.   P.M.
A.H. pitch: A   A.H. pitch: A
N.C.(A5)   A5   N.C.(A5)   Am7   To Coda
Yes, ah,   home
This is
pick sl.   1/4   A.H. (15ma)
P.M.   P.M.   sl.
sl.   P   A.H. pitch:A
N.C.(A5)   D5/A   A5   D5
the on - ly one I   know.
A.H. (15ma) 1/4   sl.   sl.
A.H. 1/4 P.M.   sl.
A.H. pitch: G

2nd Verse
w/Rhy. Fig. 1
E5   N.C.(Am)   (G)   (Am)   (G)   (E5)
An' we don't wor-ry 'bout_ to-mor-row, 'cause we're sick of these_ four_ walls.   Now
P.M.

Substitute Rhy. Fill 1
(Am)   (G)   Resume Rhy. Fig. 1   (Am)   (G)   (E5)
what you think_ is noth-in' might_ be some-thin' af-ter all._   Now you

(Am)   (G)   (Am)   (G)   (E5)
know this ain't_ no through_ street,_ the end_ is dead_ a-head._   The

(Am)   (G)   (Am)   (G)   (E5)
3
poor folks_ play for keeps down here, they're the liv-ing dead.
(Bkgd. voc.) Come on

Chorus
N.C.(A5)   Am7   N.C.(A5)   D5/A   N.C.(A5)   F5/A   F5   G5
... down,_ ah, huh! Ow!   Down_ to Mean_ Street.
down.   This is Mean_ Street.
1/4   A.H.   1/4   A.H.
(15ma)   (15ma)   1/4
1/4   P   sl.   P   P   sl.   P   sl.
P.M.   A.H.   P.M.   A.H.   P.M.   P.M.
1/4   1/4   1/4   1/4
P   P   sl.   P   P   sl.
A.H. pitch: A   A

Rhy. Fill 1
1/4
P   P   semi-harm.
1/4
P   P

N.C.(A5)
Am7
N.C.(A5)
D5/A
They're danc - in' now,
look!
Out on
Out on
Harm.
(8va)
1/4
1/4
1/4
trem. bar
A.H.
(15ma)
1/4
1/4
P
P
P
P
sl.
sl.
sl.
P.M.
A.H.
P.M.
A.H. pitch: A
A5
D5
Bridge
N.C.(A5)
Mean Street.
Dance, ba - by!
don't
pick
sl.
w/phase shifter
sl.
sl.
P
P.M.
sl.
sl.
P.M.
P.M.
P
sl.
sl.
sl.
sl.
sl.
sl.
sl.
P.M.
sl.
P.M.
P.M.
sl.
P
P
Gtr. II
(lead)
A.H.
(15ma)
rake
f
A.H.
A.H. pitch: F#
Gtr. I
(rhy.)
sl.
sl.
sl.
sl.
sl.
sl.
sl.
sl.
P.M.
P.M.
P.M.
P.M.
sl.
sl.
sl.
sl.
sl.
P
P
sl.

w/Rhy. Fig 1
A5
N.C.(D5) N.C.
C5
N.C.(Am)
(G)
It's al-ways here and now, my friend, it ain't
trem. bar
Full
Substitute Rhy. Fill 1
Resume Rhy. Fig. 1
(Am)
(G)
(E5)
(Am)
(G)
(Am)
(G)
(E5)
once up-on a time. It's all o-ver but the shout-ing, I come to take what's mine. We're
(Am)
(G)
(Am)
(G)
(E5)
search-in' for the lat-est thing, a break in this rou-tine.
D.S. al Coda
(Am)
(G)
(Am)
(G)
(E5)
Talk-in' some new kicks, ones like you ain't nev-er seen. This is
Coda
D5/A
A5
D5
E5
on-ly one I know!
(Bkgd. voc.) This is
A.H. 1/4
(15ma)
P.M.
A.H.
pitch: G

Interlude
Am7
D/A
(Spoken) See, a gun is real_ eas-y ___   in this des-p'rate part of town..
home.
This is Mean_ Street.
p
trem. bar
(slight vib.)
< mp
*(off) < mp
*Fade in w/vol. control.
Am7
3
3
Turns_ you from_hunt-ed in-to hunt-er._   Yeah.   This is
This is home.
trem. bar
(slight vib.)
(off) < mp
D/A
Am7
You go an' hunt some-bod-y down. ___   Wait a min-ute, ah!   Some-bod-y said,_ "Fair_
Mean_ Street.
This is home.
(off) < mp > < mf
(off) < mp > < mf
D/A
warn-ing!" L-Lord, ___   Lord,_ strike_ that poor boy_ down!
This is Mean_ Street.
trem. bar
(slight vib.)
(off) < mp < mf > < mf
cresc.
(increase vol.)
f pick
sl.
sl.
sl.
17
sl.

Outro
Am7
D/A
sl.
P.M.
Am7
sl.
P.M.
sl.
P.M.
D/A
Gtr. III
Full
(off)
trem. bar
Full
Full
Full
Full
1/2
Gtr. I
sl.
Rhy. Fig. 2
P.M.
sl.
Full
Full
Full
Full
Full
D/A
Full
1/2
1/2
Full
1/2
Full
Full
Full
Full
(end Rhy. Fig. 2)
sl.
P.M.
sl.
D/A
sl.
P.M.
sl.

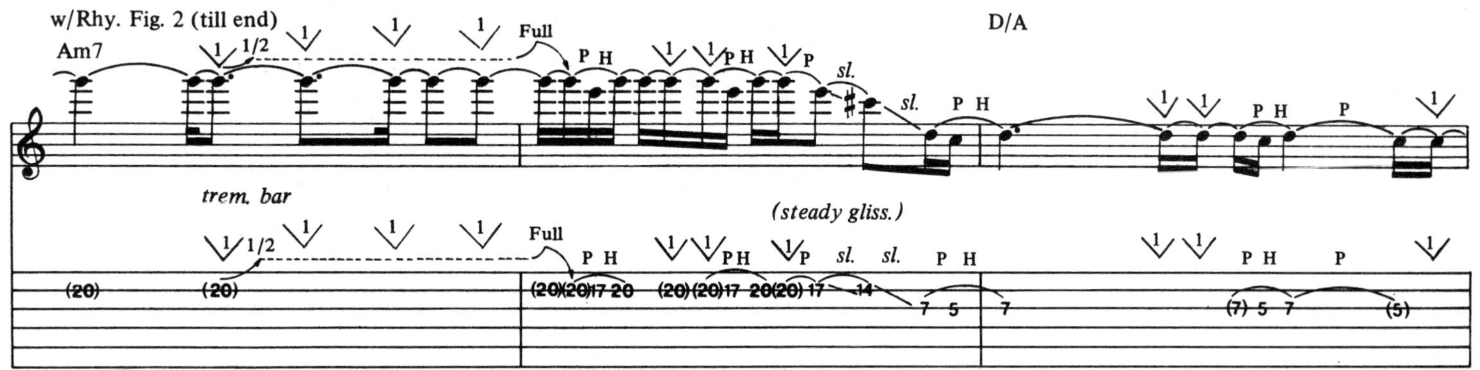

w/Rhy. Fig. 2 (till end)
Am7
D/A
Full
P H
P H
P
sl.
sl.
P H
P
trem. bar
(steady gliss.)

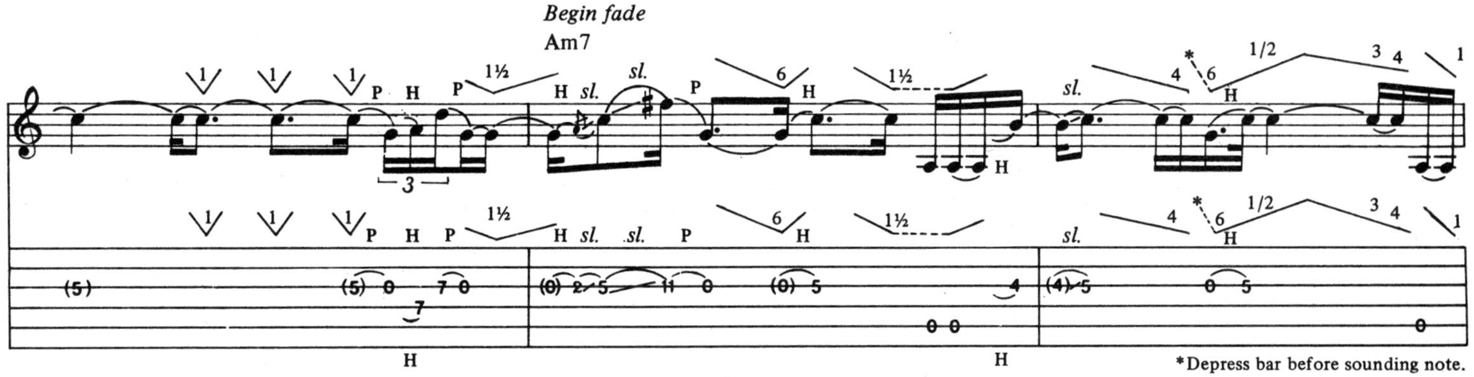

Begin fade
Am7
P H P
H sl.
sl.
P
H
H
sl.
*Depress bar before sounding note.

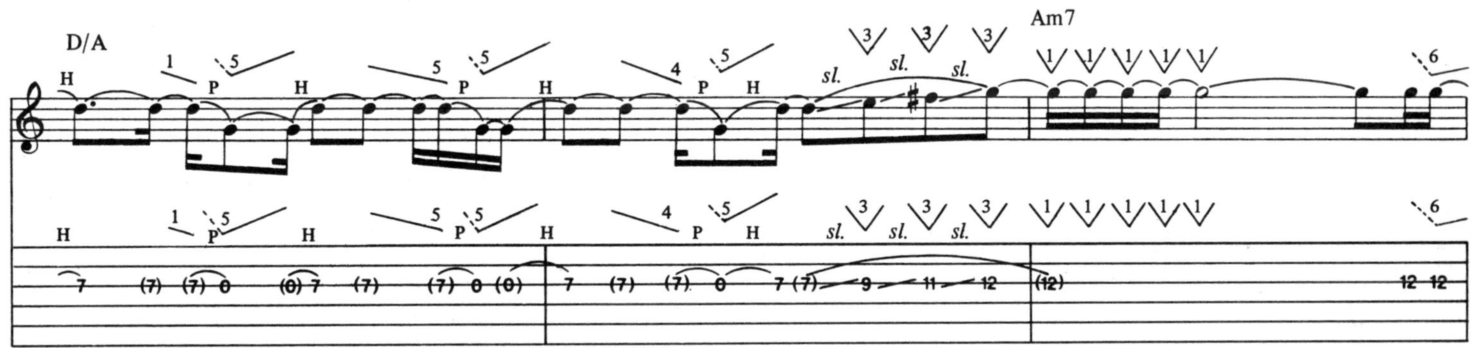

D/A
Am7
P
H
P
H
P H
sl.
sl.
sl.

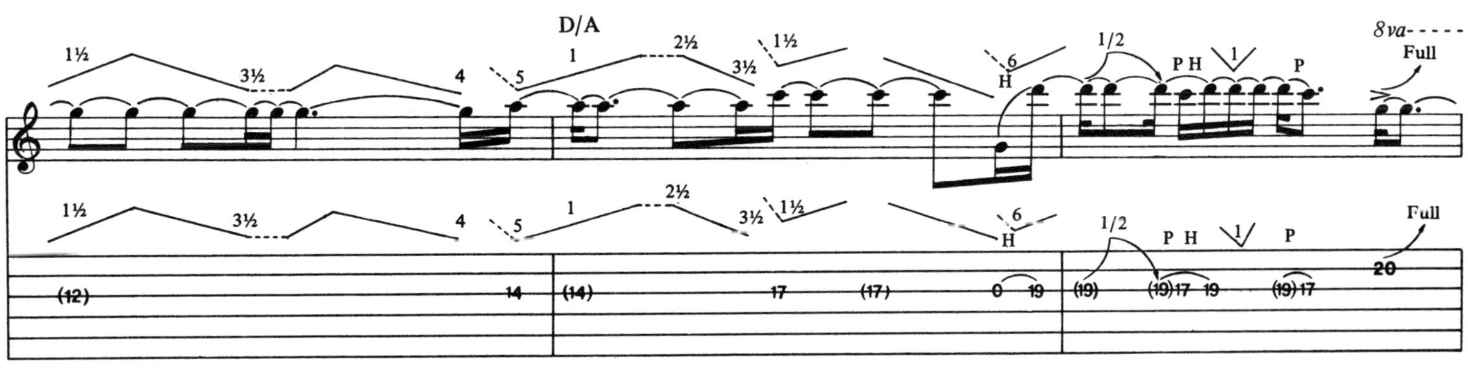

D/A
P H
P
8va
Full

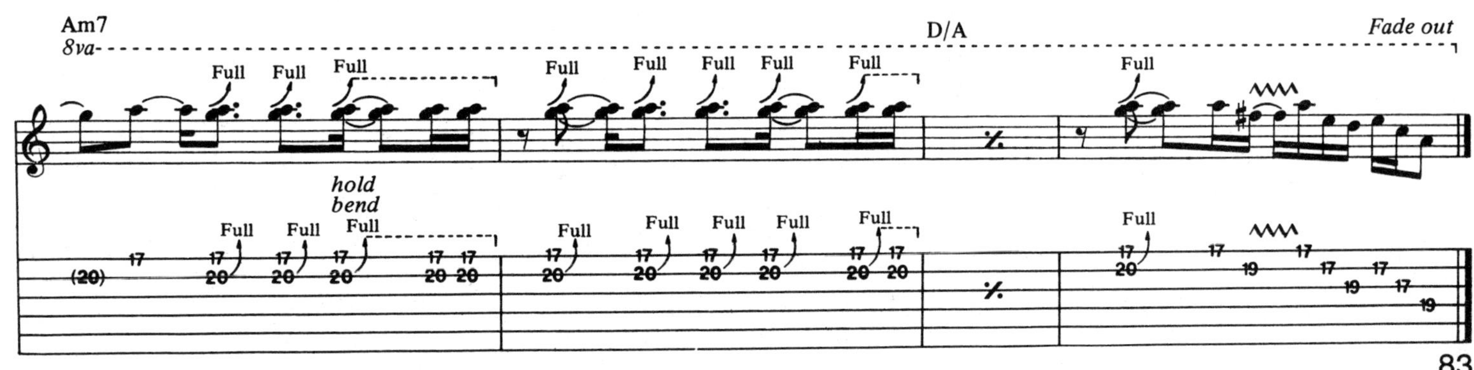

Am7
D/A
Fade out
8va
Full Full Full
Full Full Full Full Full
Full
hold
bend
Full Full Full
Full Full Full Full Full
Full

UNCHAINED

Words and Music by
Edward Van Halen, David Lee Roth,
Alex Van Halen and Michael Anthony

84

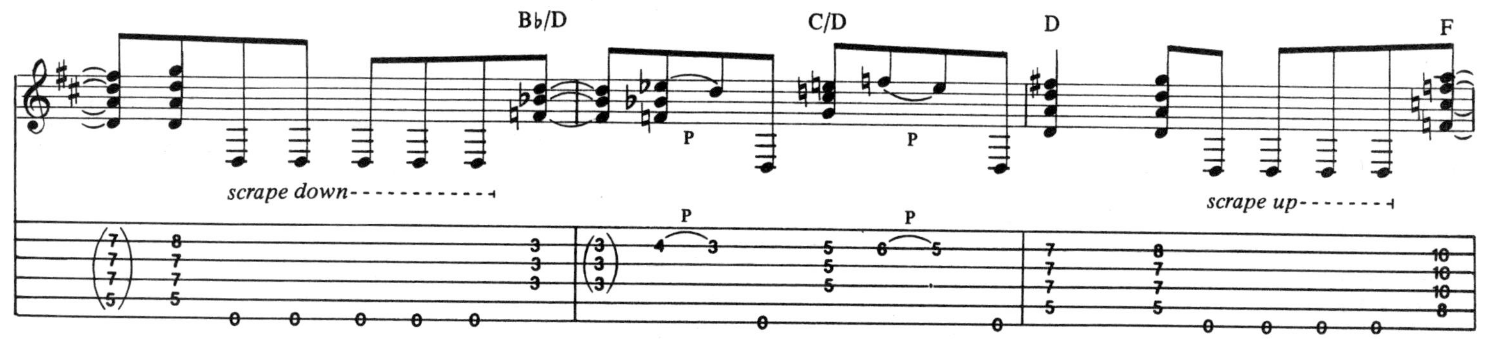

Bb/D
C/D
D
F
scrape down
P
P
scrape up

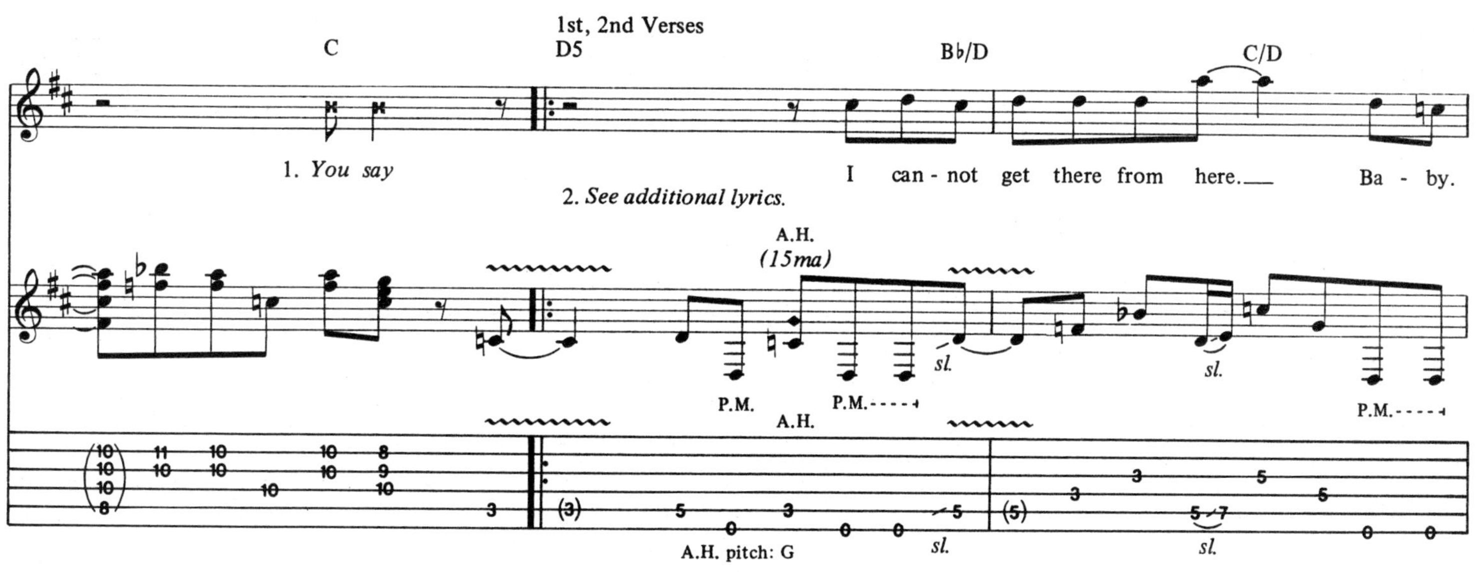

1st, 2nd Verses
C
D5
Bb/D
C/D
1. You say
2. See additional lyrics.
I can-not get there from here.___ Ba - by.
A.H.
(15ma)
P.M.
P.M.
P.M.
sl.
sl.
A.H.
A.H. pitch: G
sl.
sl.

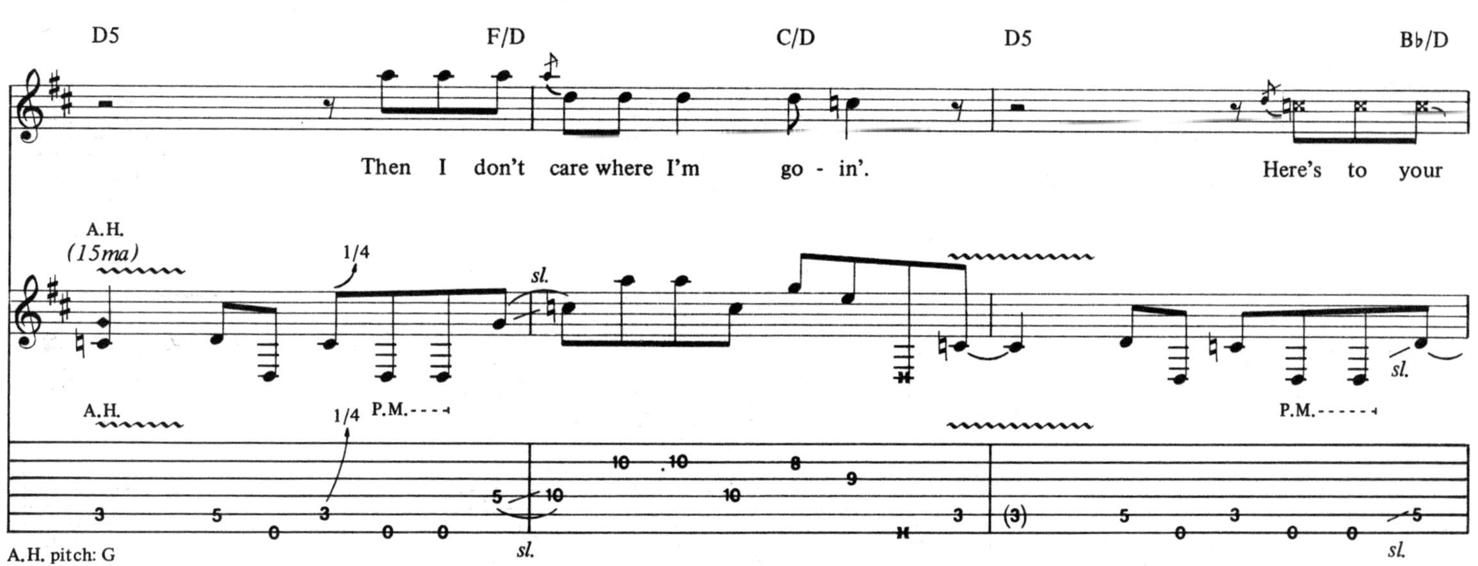

D5
F/D
C/D
D5
Bb/D
Then I don't care where I'm go - in'.
Here's to your
A.H.
(15ma)
1/4
sl.
A.H.
1/4
P.M.
P.M.
A.H. pitch: G
sl.
sl.

2nd time substitute Rhy. Fill 1
C/D
D5
F/D
C/D
thin red line.
Mm.
I'm step-ping o-ver.
A.H.
(15ma)
sl.
sl.
sl.
A.H.
A.H. pitches: G   G
Pre-chorus
G5
G5/F
Thought you'd nev-er miss me till I got a fat cit-y ad-dress.
Harm.
(8va)
Harm.
(8va)
Harm.
(8va)
sl.   sl.
sl.   sl.
Harm.
Harm.
sl.   sl.
Harm.
sl.   sl.
A5
A5/G
A5
Non-stop talk-er.   What a rock-er.   Blue-eyed mur-der in a
Harm.
(8va)
Harm.
(8va)
Harm.
(8va)
Harm.
(8va)
sl.   sl.
Harm.
Harm.
Harm.
sl.   sl.
Harm.
sl.
Rhy. Fill 1
A.H.
(15ma)
sl.
A.H.

Chorus
Ab5   G5   F5   D   Bb/D   C/D
size   five   dress.____   Change.___   Noth-in' stays____ the same.   Un - chained.___
scrape up----------
D   F   C   D   Bb/D
And you hit___ the ground   run-nin'.   Change.___   Ain't noth-in'
scrape down------   scrape up--------
C/D   D   F   C
1.
stays the same.   Un - chained.___   Yeah, you hit___ the ground   run-nin'.
2. I know!
scrape down------

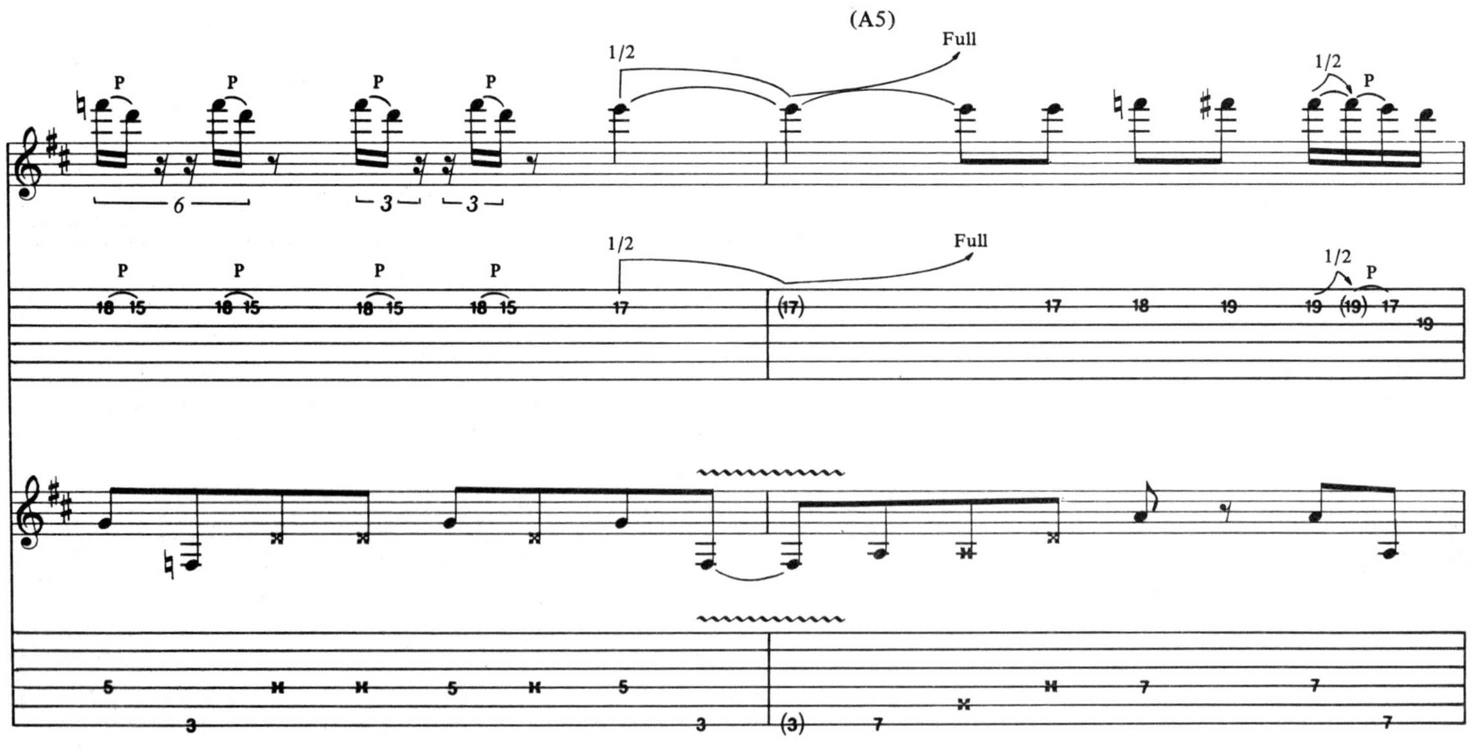
2.
C
Guitar solo
N.C.(G5)
(F5)
the ground run - nin'.
Gtr. II
Harm. (8va)
2½
Harm. (8va)
H
TP H TP H TP TP P
1/2
A.H. (15ma)
6
6
trem. bar
Harm.
2½
Harm.
H
TP H TP H TP TP P
1/2
A;H.
A.H. pitch: G
(Gtr. I)
sl.
sl.
(A5)
Full
P P P P
1/2
Full
1/2 P
P P P P
1/2
Full
1/2 P
6
3 3

(G5)
(A5)
sl. sl.
8va
Full Full
Ab5 G5 F5 D Chorus Bb/D C/D
Change. Noth-in' stays the same. Un - chained
8va
Full
(Gtr. II out)
scrape up
D F C D Bb/D
Yeah, you hit the ground run - nin'. Change. Ain't noth - in'

w/Fill 1
C/D   D   F   C
stays the same.   Un - chained   Yeah, you hit   the ground   run - nin'.
P   P   P   P

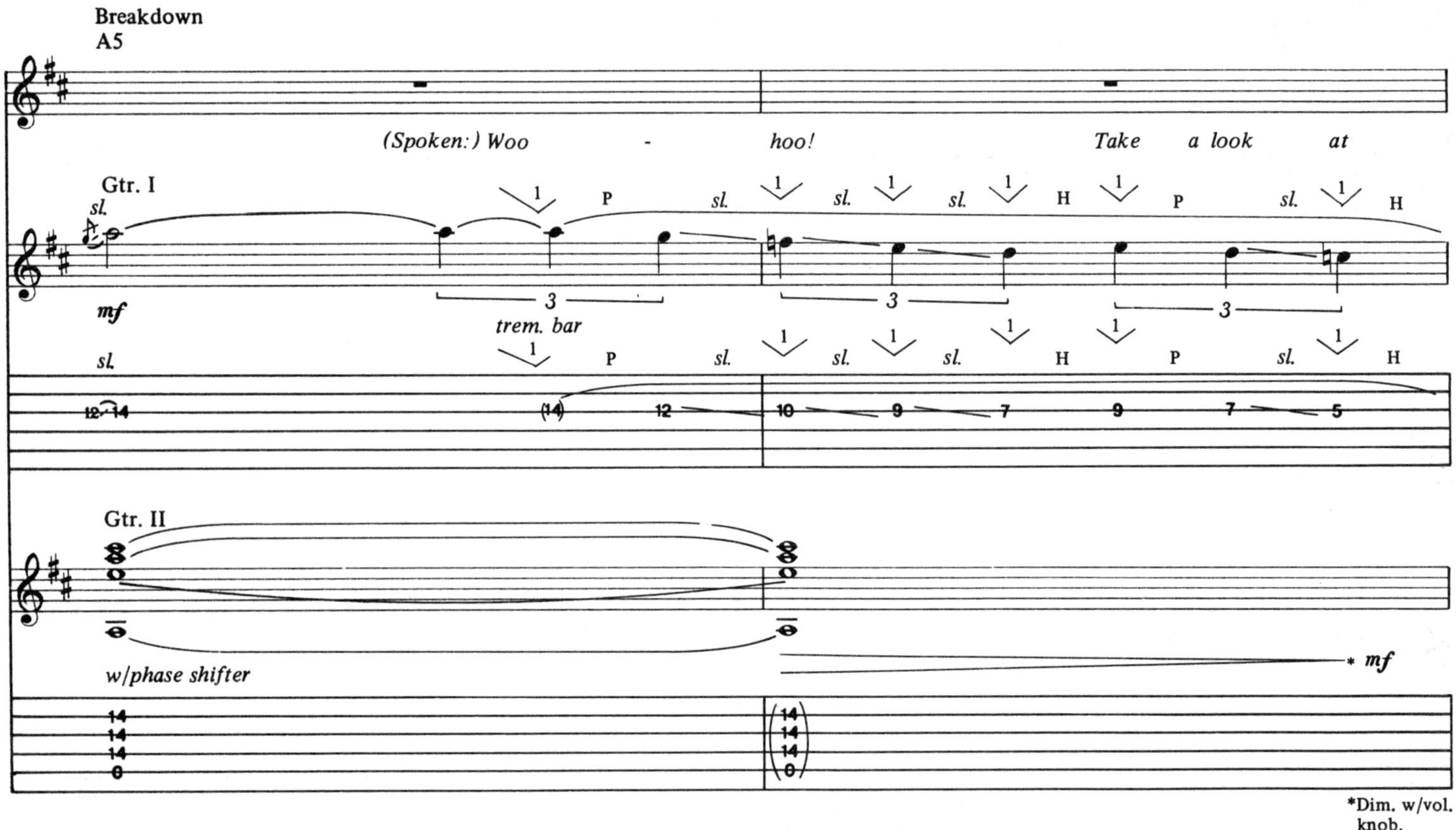

Breakdown
A5
(Spoken:) Woo - hoo!   Take a look at
Gtr. I
sl.
mf
trem. bar
sl.
Gtr. II
w/phase shifter
* mf
*Dim. w/vol. knob.

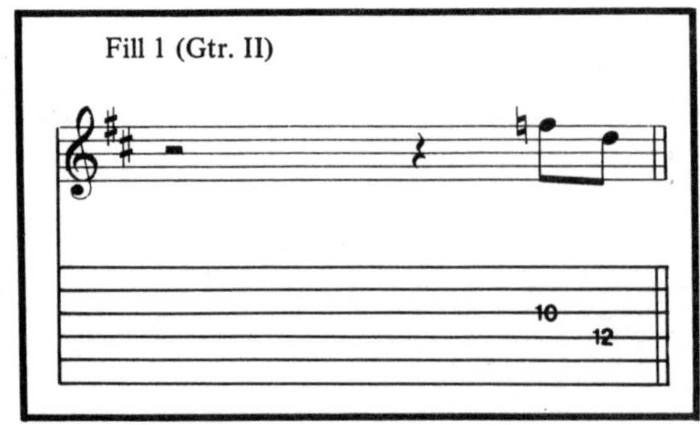

Fill 1 (Gtr. II)

G/A
D/A
A5(7)
this!
Hey man, that suit is you! Hoo - wee!
sl
P
3
sl
P
3
3
3
3

A5
A5(7)
You'll get some leg tonight for sure! Tell us how
H
3
3
mp
H
P H P H P
sl.
don't
pick
sl.
P H P H P

D/A
A5(7)
A5
you do! Hoo - hoo - hoo - hoo. (Come on, Dave, gimme a break.) Heh - heh - heh - hey.
(Gtr. I out)
P
sl. sl. sl. P sl. sl. H sl.
P
sl. sl.
17 15 17
14 12 12 11
14 16 14 12 11 8 7
A.H.
*T *T *T
sl. P sl. sl. H sl.
H
3 3
3
3
H
*T *T *T
7 7 8 7
7(19) 7(19) 7(19) 7
0
0 0 0 0 2
7 7 7
7(19) 7(19) 7(19) 7
2 2 2 2 2
*Tapped harmonic.
Gtr.
I *sl. *sl. *sl.
D
One break, comin' up!
Change...
P.M.
cresc.
f
(2/2)
2 2 2 2 2
2 2 2 2 2 2 7
2 2 2 2 2 2 7
0 0 0 0 0 0 0 0 0 0 5
*Pick slide.
Chorus
Bb/D
C/D
D
F
Ain't noth - in' stays the same. Un - chained.___ Yeah, you hit___
P
P
P
P
scrape up-----------
scrape up--------
(7) 8
3
(3) 4 3 5 6 5 7 8 10
7 7 3 3 5 5 7 7 10
7 3 3 5 5 7 7 10
(5) 5
0 0 0 0 0 0 0 0 0 5 8

C
D
Bb/D
C/D
the ground run - nin'. Change. Ain't noth - in' stays the same. Un - chained.
Riff A
scrape up
D
w/Fill 2
F
C
w/Riff A
D
Bb/D
Yeah, you hit the ground run - nin'. Change. Ain't noth - in'
(end Riff A)
Gtr. I
sl.
scrape up
sl.
C/D
D
F
C
stays the same. Un - chained. Yeah, you hit the ground run - nin'. Change.
sl.
sl.
sl.
Full
P H
Full
sl.
sl.
sl.
sl.
sl.
Full
P H
Full
Fill 2 (Gtr. I)
sl.
sl.
sl.

D
Bb/D
C/D
Ain't noth-in' stays the___ same. Un - chained___
(Gtr. I)
1/2
P H T P H P TP P H TP P H T P P H T P P H TP P
1/2
P H T P H P TP P H TP P H T P P H T P P H TP P
13 (13) 10 13 15 13 10 13 17 13 10 13 15 13 10 13 17 13 10 13 15 13 10 12 14 12 10
Gtr. II
7 8 3
7 7 3
7 7 3
5 5
3 3 4 5 6 5
(3) 3 5 5
(3) 3 5 5
0 0 0 0 0 0
P
D
F C F C F
sl.
H
1/4 1/2
sl. sl. sl.
sl.
Full
P.M.
sl.
sl. sl. sl.
Full
1/4 1/2
(10) 10 10 10 9 12 9 10 (10) 10 10 9 13 13
10 10 10 10 10 10 10 10
12 12 8 (8) 8 8 7
sl. H
sl. sl.
7 8 10 10 10 10 8 10 (10) 10 10 10 10 8 11
7 7 10 10 10 10 9 10 10 10 10 10 9 10
7 7 10 10 10 10 10 10 (10) 10 10 10 10 10 10
5 8 (8) 8
0 0 0 0 0 0 0

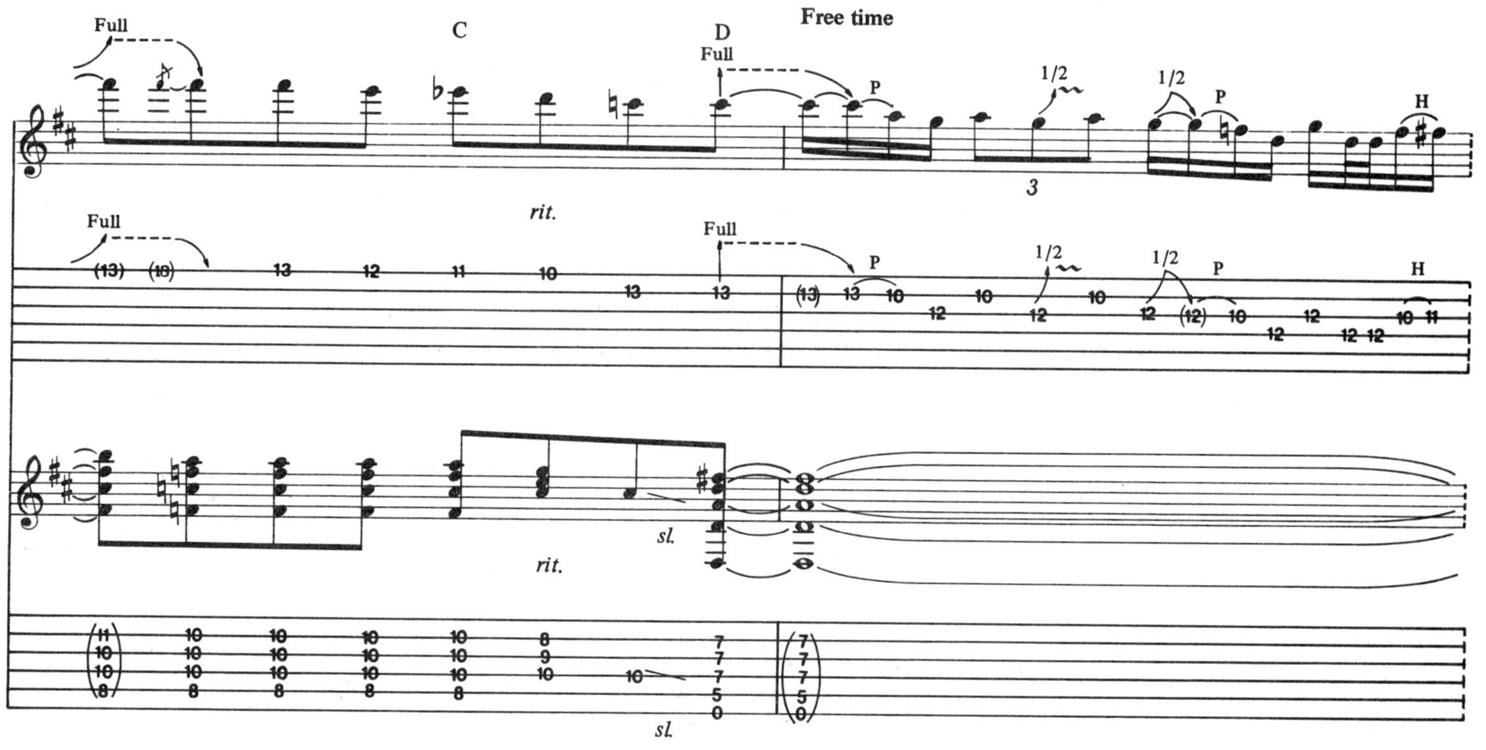

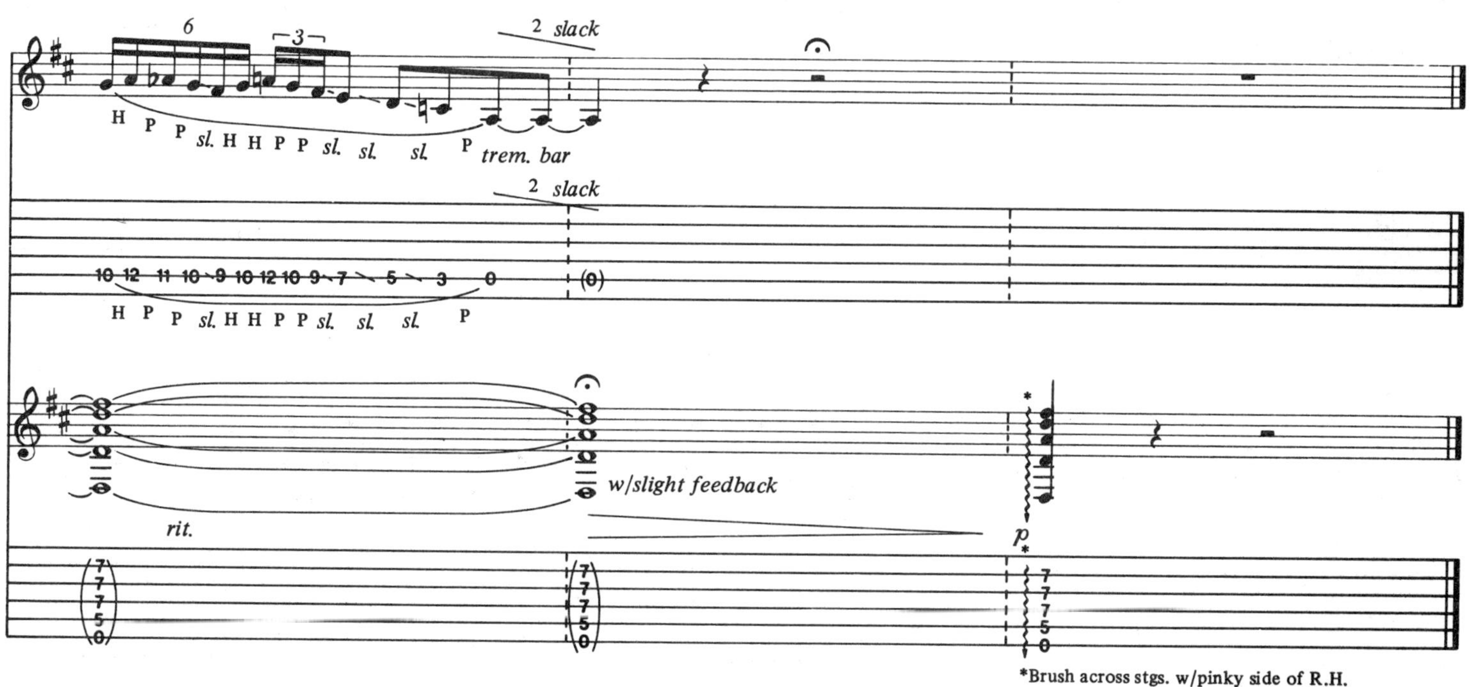

Additional Lyrics

2. I know I don't ask for permission.
This is my chance to fly.
Maybe enough ain't enough for you,
But it's my turn to try. *(To Pre-chorus)*

CATHEDRAL

Music by Edward Van Halen,
Alex Van Halen, Michael Anthony
and David Lee Roth

LITTLE GUITARS (INTRO)

Music by Edward Van Halen,
Alex Van Halen, Michael Anthony,
and David Lee Roth

LITTLE GUITARS

Words and Music by
Edward Van Halen, Alex Van Halen,
Michael Anthony and David Lee Roth

Fmaj7 sus#4 sus2
let ring
P.M.
P.M.
P.M.
Double time ♩ = 144
B5
let ring
let ring
F/A
A7sus4
A7
(flanger off)
1st Verse
D
Csus2
Se - ño - ri - ta, I'm in trou - ble a - gain___ and I can't get___ free.
Rhy. Fig. 1
*w/fingers
w/fingers
*Hold pick with thumb and index finger
and pick with middle and ring fingers.
D
You're ex - act - ly what the doc - tor or - dered. Come on,
(Se - no - ri - ta.)
w/fingers

Csus2
Fsus#4 sus2
F
talk to me.
Can't grow be-fore I'm
(Ah.
(end Rhy. Fig. 1) Rhy. Fig. 2
w/fingers
w/fingers
Fsus#4 sus2
F
Fsus#4 sus2
F
Fsus#4 sus2
F
out of the woods, but there's ex-cep-tions to the rule.
Ah.)
(end Rhy. Fig. 2)
w/fingers
w/fingers
H
H
Half time feel
A7sus4
A9
A7sus4
A7
(end half time feel)
Se-ño-ri-ta, do you need a friend? I'm in love with you.
let ring
w/flanger
(flanger off)
Chorus
G Gsus#4 G5
G Gsus#4 G5
G Gsus#4 G5
G Gsus#4 G5
Catch as catch, catch as catch can. An-y-bod-y in their right mind could
Rhy. Fig. 3
(end Rhy. Fig. 3)
P.M. P.M. P.M.
P.M. P.M. P.M.
P.M. P.M. P.M.

w/Rhy. Fig. 1
D
Csus2
see   it's you   and ___ me.
D
Csus2
Ooh.
Ooh.
2nd Verse
w/Rhy. Fig. 2
Fsus2sus#4
F
Fsus2sus#4
F
Fsus2sus#4
F
Fsus2sus#4
F
You say you're lone-some, just get - ting by, ___ but you turn your eyes ___ from ___ me.
Half time feel
A7sus4
A9
A7sus4
A7
(end half time feel)
Please, se - ño - ri - ta, be - fore you ___ fly, 'cause you've got ___ me.
let ring
w/flanger
(flanger off)
Chorus
w/Rhy. Fig. 3
G Gsus#4 G5
G
Gsus#4 G5
G Gsus#4 G5
G Gsus#4 G5
Catch as catch, catch ___ as catch ___ can.   An - y - bod - y in their ___ right ___ mind ___ can ___
D
see ___   you and ___   me.
w/fingers

G Gsus#4 G5 G Gsus#4 G5 G Gsus#4 G5 G Gsus#4 G5
Catch as catch, catch as catch can. When I see you, all your lit - tle gui - tars
P P
P.M. P.M. P.M. P.M. P.M. P.M. P.M. P.M. P.M.
Half time feel
A7sus4 A7 A7sus4 A7
sing to me.
let ring
w/flanger
Guitar solo
Gsus#4
Gtr. II
A7sus4 A7
w/slide steady gliss.
w/flanger & delay steady gliss. steady gliss.
Gtr. I
let ring

Gsus#4
A7sus4
A7
P.M.
steady gliss.
steady gliss.
steady gliss.
(flanger off)
G5 Gsus#4 G5 N.C.
(Gtr. II out)
(end half time feel)
steady gliss.
P.M.
sl.
sl.
sl.
sl.
sl.
sl.
3rd Verse
w/Rhy. Fig. 1
D
Csus2
I can see you don't know which way to turn,___ but the sun still___ shines.
D
Don't you know that you can dance with me___
(Se - ño - ri - ta.)
Csus2
w/Rhy. Fig. 2
Fsus#4sus2
F
Can't grow be - fore I'm
an - y - time?
Fsus#4sus2
F
Fsus#4sus2
F
(Ah.
Fsus#4sus2
F
out of the woods;__ there's ex - cep - tions to the___ rule.
Ah.)

Half time feel
A7sus4
A7
A7sus4
A7
(end half time feel)
Se - ño - ri - ta, do you need a friend? I'm in love with you.
let ring
w/flanger
P.M.
(flanger off)
w/Rhy. Fig. 3
G Gsus♯4 G5 G Gsus♯4 G5 G Gsus♯4 G5 G
Gsus♯4 G5
Gtr. III
w/Rhy. Fig. 1 (1st 4 bars only, 4 times)
D
pick slide
w/fingers
Csus2
w/fingers
P.M.
D
Csus2
Ooh.
Ooh.
w/fingers
pick
slide
H sl.
w/fingers
H sl.
sl.
sl.

D
Csus2
Ooh.
Ooh.
sl.
P
w/fingers-
w/fingers-
sl.
sl.
D
Csus2
Ooh.
Ooh.
w/fingers-
w/fingers-
Gtr. I
Csus2
1.
w/fingers-
w/fingers-
Gtr. III
(Gtr. III out)
(Play 1st time only)
2.
D
Csus2
w/fingers-

JUMP

Words and Music by
Edward Van Halen, Alex Van Halen,
Michael Anthony and David Lee Roth

(1st,) 2nd Verses
w/Riff A (2 times)
G/C   C   F/C   G/C   C   F/C   C/F   Gsus4
are you?_ Who said that?   ba - by, just_ how you_ feel._   You got to
G/C   C   F/C   G/C   C   F/C   C/F   Gsus4
roll_____ with the punch-es   to get to what's real._   Ah, can't you
know,_____ you won't_ know_   un-til you be - gin._   So, can't you
Pre-chorus
N.C.(Am)   (F)   (C/E)   (Dm)
see me stand-in' here? I got my back a-gainst the rec-ord ma-chine._____
Gtr. II
slight vib. w/bar
P.M.
sl.
(F)   (C/E)   (Dm)
I ain't the worst that you've seen._____   Ah, can't you see what I mean?_
slight vib. w/bar
P.M.   P.M.
sl.   sl.
(F)   (C/E)   (G)
Ah,   might as well_ jump._
(Gtr. II out)
slight vib. bar
P.M.
sl.

Chorus
w/Riff A
(Jump!)
1. Might as well jump.
2. Go a-head and jump.
Go a-head and jump.
Might as well jump.
1st time w/Riff A1
2nd time w/Riff A
(Jump!)
Go a-head and jump.
2. How old Jump!
Guitar solo
*Bbm
**Gtr. III
rake
rake
semi-harm.
*Chord names derived from bass and synth. (next 8 bars).
**Tune down 1/2 step. Music sounds as written.
Riff A1
Gtr. I

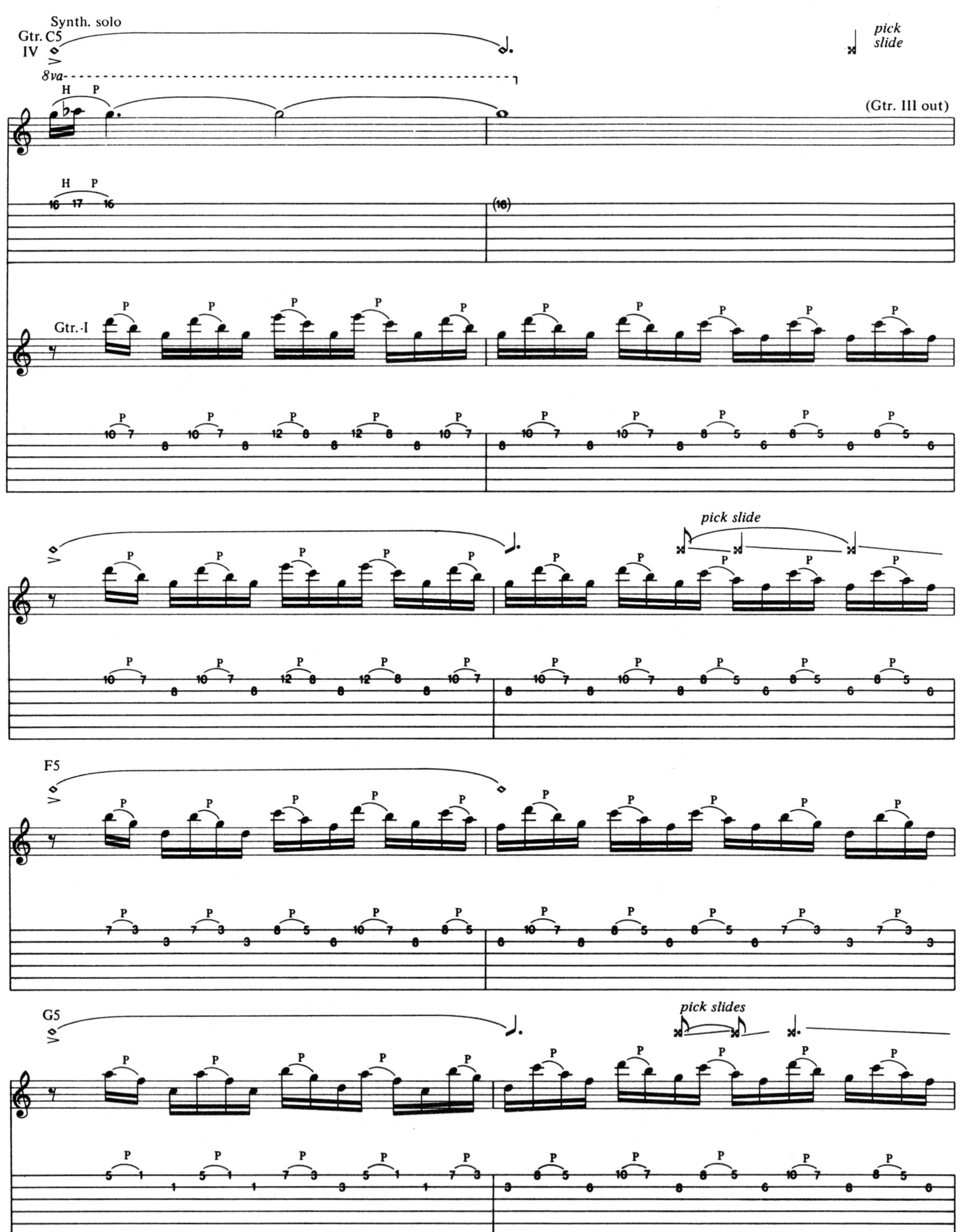

Synth. solo
Gtr. C5
IV
pick
slide
8va
H P
(Gtr. III out)
H P
16 17 16
(16)
Gtr. I
P
10 7 10 7 8 12 8 12 8 10 7 8 10 7 8 5 6 8 5 6
pick slide
10 7 10 7 12 8 12 8 10 7 10 7 10 7 8 5 8 5 8 5 6
F5
7 3 7 3 3 8 5 6 10 7 8 6 10 7 8 5 6 6 3 7 3
G5
pick slides
5 1 5 1 1 7 3 5 1 3 3 8 5 10 7 8 5 6 10 7 8 5 6

Bb5
pick slide
8va
H H *T
*T =Tap w/R.H. index finger.
=Tap w/R.H. ring finger.
=Pull-off to R.H. index finger.
Asus4
8va
pick slide
Absus2
8va
9:8
G5
loco
C5
(Gtr. IV out)
w/Riff A
G/C   C   F/C   G/C   C   F/C   1. C/F Gsus4   2. C/F Gsus4
Out-chorus
w/Riff A (3 times)
G/C   C   F/C   G/C   C   F/C   C/F Gsus4
Might as well
jump. (Jump!)   Go a-head and   jump.   Get in and
Gtr. II
P.M.

G/C   C   F/C   G/C   C   F/C   C/F   Gsus4
jump. (Jump!)   Go a-head and   jump.   Jump!
P.M.   P.M.
G/C   C   F/C   G/C   C   F/C   C/F   Gsus4
Jump!   Jump!
Begin fade
w/Riff B
F/C   C   F/C   C/F   Gsus4   w/Riff A   G/C   C
Jump!
P.M.   P.M.   P.M.
F/C   G/C   C   F/C   C/F   Gsus4   w/Riff B   F/C   Fade out   C
P.M.

PANAMA

Words and Music by
Edward Van Halen, Alex Van Halen,
Michael Anthony and David Lee Roth

Moderate Rock ♩ = 144
Intro
Gtr. I
E   Esus4   B/E   E   Esus4   B/E   D   Dsus4   A
f   P.M.
sl.
E   Esus4   B/E   E   Esus4   B/E
rake   trem. bar
P.M.
D   Dsus4   A   C#m
sl.   P.M.   pick sl.   let ring   P.M.
B/C#   B A   A.H. Full (15ma)   C#5
P   P.M.   sl.   A.H. Full   let ring
A.H.
pitch: A
B/C#   B A   B   Harm.-- (8va)
H   P   sl.   N.C.
P.M.   Harm.--

N.C. A5 D5 A5 D5 A5 N.C.
Harm.
(8va)
Oo!
Oh,—
Harm.
* Harm. on 3rd stg., 4th fret.
P.M.
P.M.
P.M.
P.M.
P.M.
sl. sl.
sl. sl.
A5 D A D A N.C.
A5 D A D A N.C.
yeah!
Uh,— huh!
P.M.
P.M.
P.M.
sl. sl.
sl. sl.
1st Verse
A5 D A D A N.C.
E5
A/E
Jump back! What's that sound?—
P.M.
P.M.
P.M.
sl. sl.
1/2 1/2 1/2
trem. bar
1/2 1/2 1/2
sl. sl.
E7sus4
E5
A/E
Here she comes,— full blast and top down. Hot shoe, burn - in' down the av - e - nue.
P.M.

E7sus4
F#sus4
F#7add4
Mod - el cit - i - zen, ze - ro dis - ci - pline. Don't you know she's com - in' home to me?
let ring
pick.slides
C#m7
B5
You'll lose her in the turn. I'll get her!
pick.sl. sl.
N.C.
Chorus
N.C.
N.C. A D5 A D5 A N.C.
Pan - a - ma,
Pan - a - ma.
Harm. (15ma)
Harm. (8va)
P.M.
Harm.
Harm.
A5 D A5 D5 A N.C. A D A D5 A N.C.
Pan - a - ma,
Pan - a - ma.
sim.
P.M.
sl. sl.
sl. sl.

2nd Verse
A D A D5 A N.C.
E5
A/E
Ain't noth-in' like it, her shin-y ma-chine,___ got the
P.M. P.M. P.M.
P.M.
sl. sl.
P.M. P.M.
sl. sl.
E7sus4
E5
A/E
feel for the wheel, keep the mov-ing parts clean.
Hot shoe,___ burn-in' down the av-e-nue,
P.M.
E7sus4
F#7sus4
F#7add4
got an on ramp com-in' through my bed-room.
Don't you know she's com-in' home___ to me?___
let ring
pick slides
let ring
P.M.
let ring
sl.
sl.
C#m7
3
N.C.
C5 N.C.
B5
You'll lose her in the___ turn.___
I'll get her!
let ring
sl.
sl.
14
sl.

Chorus
Wuh__ oh!
Pan - a - ma,
Pan - a - ma.
Ow!__
Pan - a - ma,
Pan - a - ma
ah oh__ oh__ oh__ oh.
Guitar solo
Woo!__
* Chords derived from bass figure.
117

Interlude
Yeah, we're run-nin' a lit-tle bit hot to-night.
I can bare-ly see the road from the heat com-in' off it.

C(b5)   C5   E5
Ah, _______ you reach down _______ be - tween my
P.M. P.M.
sl. sl. sl.
P.M. P.M. P.M.

C(b5)   C5   C(b5)   C5
legs, _______
ease   the   seat   back.
P.M. P.M.
sl.

E5   F   D/F#   G5   E/G#
She's blind-in',   I'm fly-in',   right be-hind in the rear - view mir-ror now.
P.M. P.M. P.M. P.M.

A5   Gm/Bb   B5   B
Got the feel-ing,   pow-er steer-ing,   pis-tons pop-pin', ain't no stop-ping now!
P.M.

Chorus
N.C. A5 D A D A N.C. A D A
Pan - a - ma. Pan - a - ma.
P.M. P.M. P.M. sl. sl. sim.
sl. sl.
D A N.C. A5 D5 A D A N.C. A5 D A5
Pan - a - ma, Pan - a - ma ah oh oh oh
sl. sl. sl. sl. sl. sl.
D A N.C. A5 D A5 D A N.C.
oh. Pan - a - ma, Pan - a - ma
sl. sl. sl. sl. P.M.
sl. sl.
A5 Dsus2 A D A N.C.
ah oh oh oh oh. Pan - a - ma.
P.M. P.M. P.M.

HOT FOR TEACHER

Words and Music by
Edward Van Halen, Alex Van Halen,
Michael Anthony and David Lee Roth

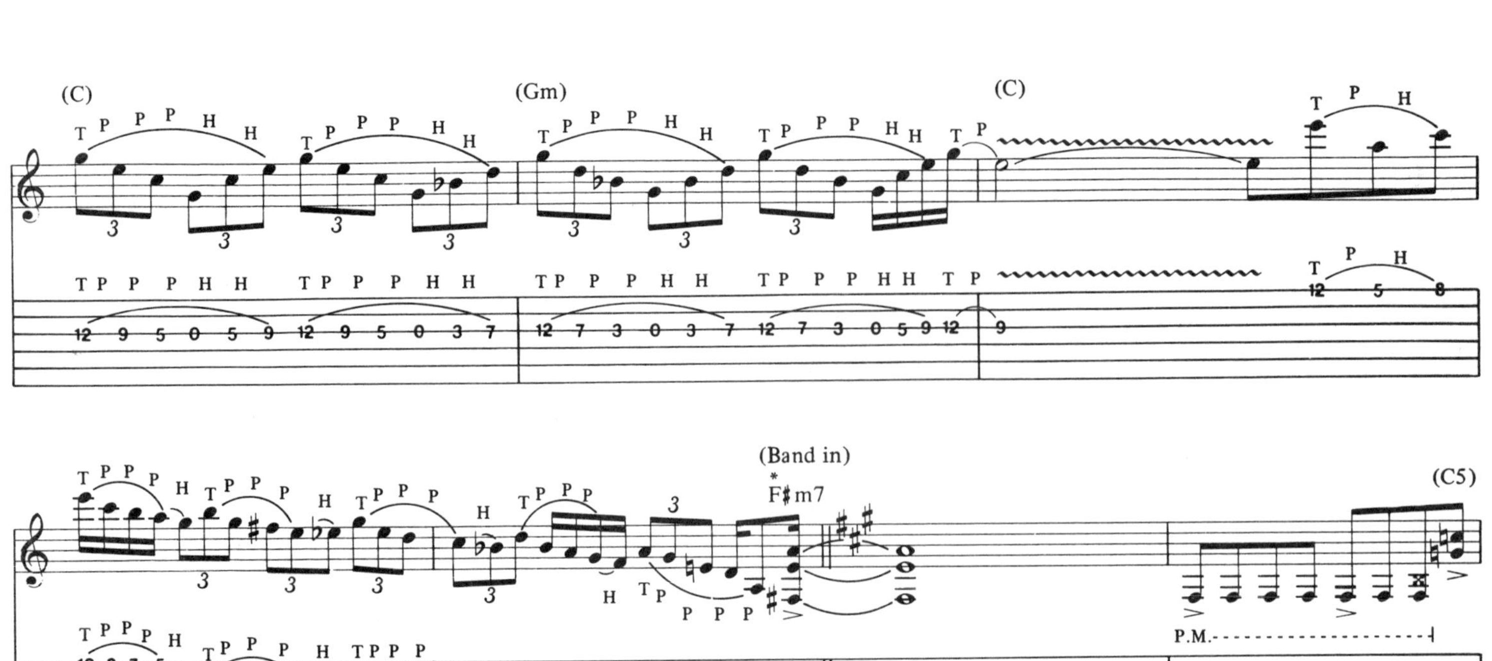

(C)
(Gm)
(C)
T P P P H H
T P P P H H
T P P P H H
T P P P H H H T P
T P H
3   3   3   3
3   3   3
T P P P H H   T P P P H H   T P P P H H   T P P P H H T P
T P H
12 9 5 0 5 9 12 9 5 0 3 7
12 7 3 0 3 7 12 7 3 0 5 9 12   9
12   5   8

(Band in)
*
F#m7
(C5)
T P P P H T P P P H T P P P   T P P P   3
H T P
P P P
P.M.
T P P P H   T P P P   P   H   T P P P
12 8 7 5   8 12 8 7 5   8 12 8 7   5   2
2
5
8 12 8 7 5   2
5
8 12 8 7 5 0   2
H T P P P H   T P P P P   2
2 2 2 2 2 2 2
*Bass plays F# pedal.

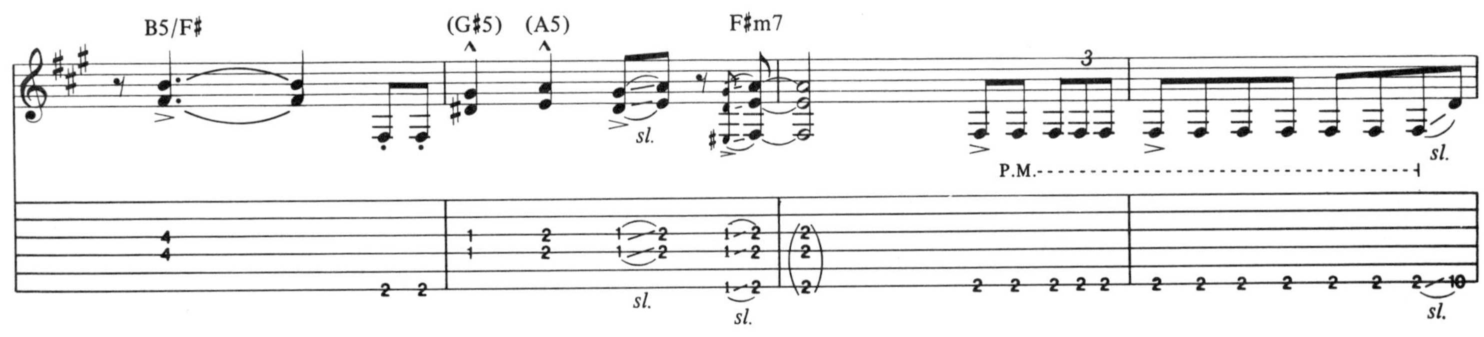

B5/F#
(G#5) (A5)
F#m7
3
sl.
P.M.
4
1   2   2   1 2
4
1   2   1 2   2
sl.
2 2   1 2   2   2 2 2 2 2   2 2 2 2 2 2 2 2 10
2 2   sl.
sl.   1 2   (2)   sl.
sl.

(F5)   (D5)   B5/F#   (G#5)   (A5)   F#m7   (C5)
sl.
sl.   sl.   sl.
sl.   sl.   sl.   P.M.
10   (10) 7   (7) 4   (4)   1   2   1   2   5
10   (10) 7   (7) 4   (4)   1   2   2   5
sl.   sl.   2 2 2 2 2   2 2 2 2 2 2 2 2

B5/F#   (G#5)   (A5)   Esus4
sl.
*(w/fingers)
mp
4   4 4   1   2   1 2   2   2   2   (2) 2   2   2
4   4 4   1   2   1 2   2   2   2   2 2   2   0
2   0   0   0   (0)   0
sl.

*Flick toggle switch on two pickup/two volume
control guitar to neck pickup w/volume
rolled down for attenuation & cleaner tone.
Ed uses Gibson Flying V for this purpose
for entire track.

Am7
D5   Am7
(Classroom noise/chaos)
(Spoken) 2. Hey, I heard you missed us,
(Spoken) 1. Oh we're back.
I think the clock is slow.
3
sl.
P   P   P
H H H
P
5 2 5 2 2 2 (2) 5 5 2 2 2 (2) 5 2 5 8 7 2
2 2 2 2 2 2 (2) 2 2 2 2 2 (2) 2 5 8 7 2
0 5 6 7
H H H   sl.

2nd time w/Rhy. Fill 2
D5   Am7
wow, man, I said...
Wait a
I brought my
What are you doing this weekend?
3
sl.
P   P   P
H H H
P
(2) 5 5 2 2 2 (2) 5 5 2 2 2 (2) 5 2 5 8 7 2
2 2 2 2 2 2 (2) 2 2 2 2 2 (2) 2 5 8 7 2
0 5 6 7
H H H   sl.

2nd time w/Rhy. Fill 3
D5   Am7
second, man.
pencil.
I don't feel tardy.
Whatta ya think the teacher's gonna look like this
Give me somethin' to write on, man.
3
sl.
P   P   P
H H H
P
(2) 5 5 2 2 2 (2) 5 5 2 2 2 (2) 5 2 5 8 7 2
2 2 2 2 2 2 (2) 2 2 2 2 2 (2) 2 5 8 7 2
0 5 6 7
H H H   sl.

Rhy. Fill 2
1/4
3
sl.
P   P
1/4 P
H H H   sl.
P
(2) 5 5 2 2 2 (2) 5 2 5 8 7 2
2 2 2 2 2 2 (2) 2 5 8 7 2
0   0 5 6 7
H H H   sl.

Rhy. Fill 3
3
(P)
P
H H H
(2) 5 2
2 2
(0) 0 5 6 7
H H H

year?
Whoa!
Uh!
Class
dimissed!
To Coda
A5
Ooh!
*Flick toggle switch to
bridge pickup with volume
at full output.
D5
A5
Oh.
Yeah.
Ooh.
Rhy. Fig. 1
T - t - t - teach - er,
I
(end Rhy. Fig. 1)
D5
A5

1st, 2nd Verses
w/Rhy. Fig. 1 (3 times)
D5   A5
stop that screamin'. Teach - er, don't you see?
heard a - bout your les - sons, but les - sons are so cold.

2nd time substitute Rhy. Fill 4
D5   A5
Don't wan - na be no up - town fool.
I know a - bout this school. Lit -

D5   A5
May - be I should go to hell, uh, but I am do - ing well.
tle girl from Cher - ry Lawn, how can you be so bold?

w/Rhy. Fig. 1 (1st 3 bars only)
C5 Eb5 D5 C5 D5
Teach - er needs to see me af - ter school.
How did you know that gold - en rule?

5 8 7 5 7
5 8 7 5 7
5

Pre-chorus
2nd time w/Rhy. Fill 5
Ab5 G5 F5 G5
I think of all the ed - u - ca - tion that I missed,

Harm.
let ring   *Harm.   pick slides (steady gliss.)

7   7 (19)   7 (19)   13 12 10 12
7   5 (17)   7 (19)   13 12 10 12
5   5 (17)
T

*Tap harmonics. Hold chord
form while tapping harmonic
an octave (12 frets) above.
**Vib. 3rd & 4th stgs.

Rhy. Fill 4
H H
2
0 0 0   0 6 7
H H

Rhy. Fill 5
Harm.
let ring
Harm.
7   7 7   7 (7) 7
7   7
5   7   7

2nd time substitute Rhy. Fill 6
but then my home-work was nev-er quite like this.
**Vib. creates harmonics.
sl.
1/4
1/4
(both notes vib.)
sl.
2nd time substitute Rhy. Fill 7
Bb5   A5   Ab5   G5   F#5   F5   E5   Db5   E5   A5
Oh.   Got it bad,
Whoa.
sl.
Chorus
w/Rhy. Fig. 1 (3 times)
got it bad,   got it bad,   I'm hot for teach-
D5   A5
Rhy. Fill 6
pick slide (steady gliss.)
1/4
1/4
1/4
1/4
both notes vib.
sl.   sl.
sl.
Rhy. Fill 7

D5
A5
I've got it bad,
Substitute Rhy. Fill 1
Resume Rhy. Fig. 1
D5
A5
so
bad,
I'm hot for teach -
1.
Esus4
A
er.
P
P
P
P
*mf
*Switch to neck pickup.
2.
(Band tacet)
N.C.
(Band in)
*F#m
er.
Wuh,
oh.
(steady gliss.)
T P P
T P P P
H
T P P
P H
T P P P
H
T P P P
T
Full
P
P
P
P
H
Full
T P P
12 5 3
T P P P
12 8 7 5
H
T P P P H
8 12 8 7 5
T P P P H
8 12 8 7 5
8 (8)12 8 7 5
8 12 8 7 5 0
4
P
P
H
T P P H
T P P P
*Chords implied by bass.
Rhy. Fill 1
3
H H H
H H H

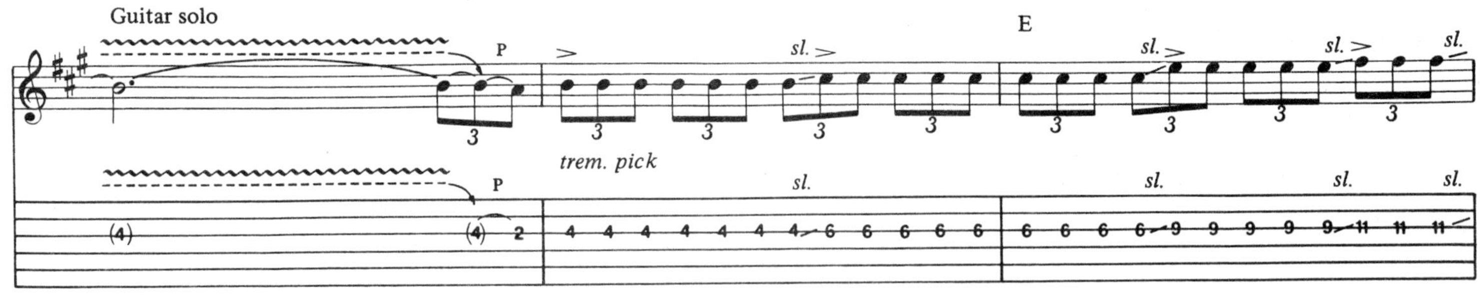

Guitar solo
P
trem. pick
sl.
E
sl.
sl.
sl.
(4)
(4)
2
4 4 4 4 4 4 4 6 6 6 6
6 6 6 6 9 9 9 9 9 11 11 11

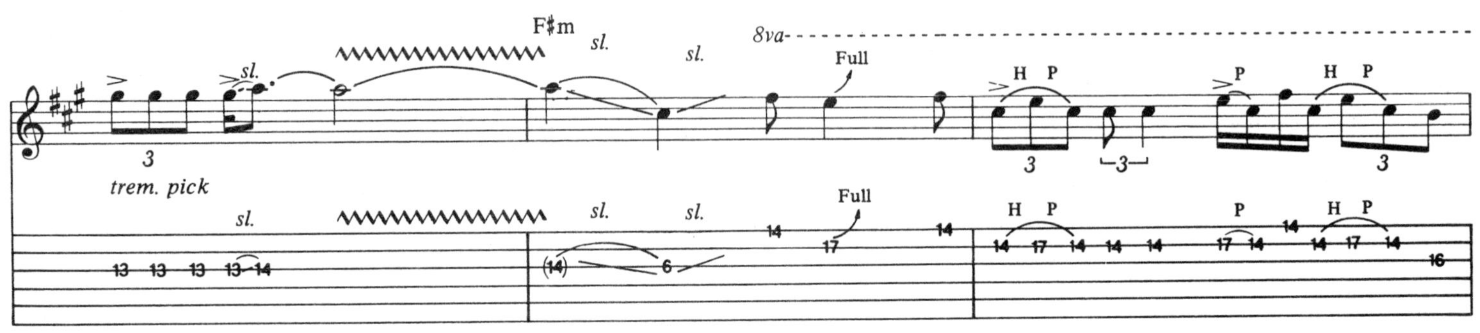

F#m
sl.
sl.
8va
Full
H P
P
H P
trem. pick
sl.
sl.
sl.
Full
H P
P
H P
3
13 13 13 13 14
(14)
6
14
17
14
14 17 14 14 14
17 14
14 17 14
16

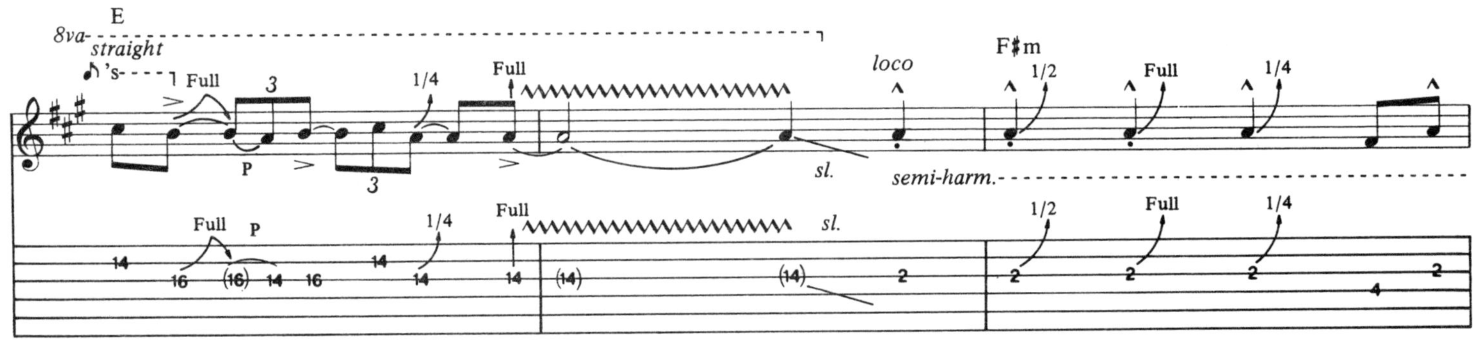

E
8va
straight
's
Full
3
1/4
Full
loco
F#m
1/2
Full
1/4
P
sl.
semi-harm.
Full P
1/4
Full
sl.
1/2
Full
1/4
14
16 (16) 14 16
14
14
(14)
(14)
2
2
2
2
4
2

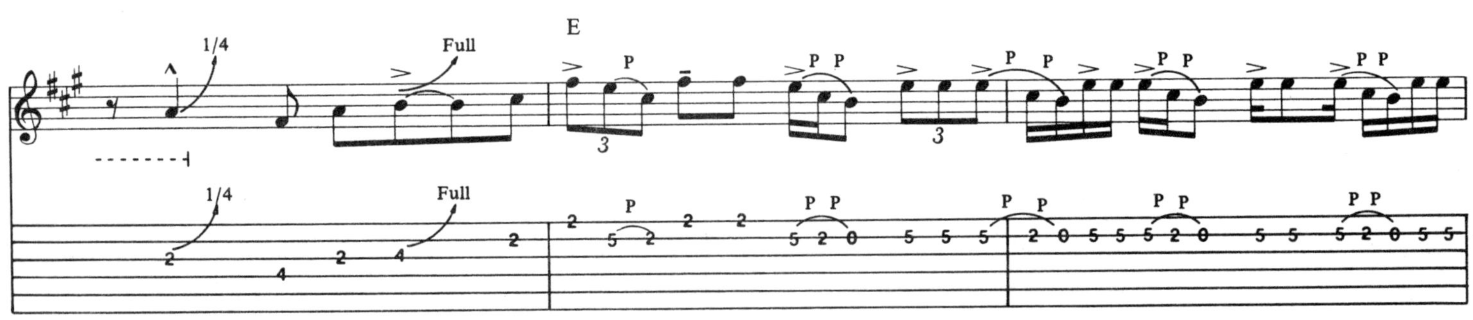

1/4
Full
E
P
P P
P P
P P
P P
P P
1/4
Full
P
P P
P P
P P
P P
1/4
Full
2
2 2 2
5 2 0
5 5 5
2 0 5 5 5 5 2 0
5 5
5 2 0 5 5
2
4
2 4

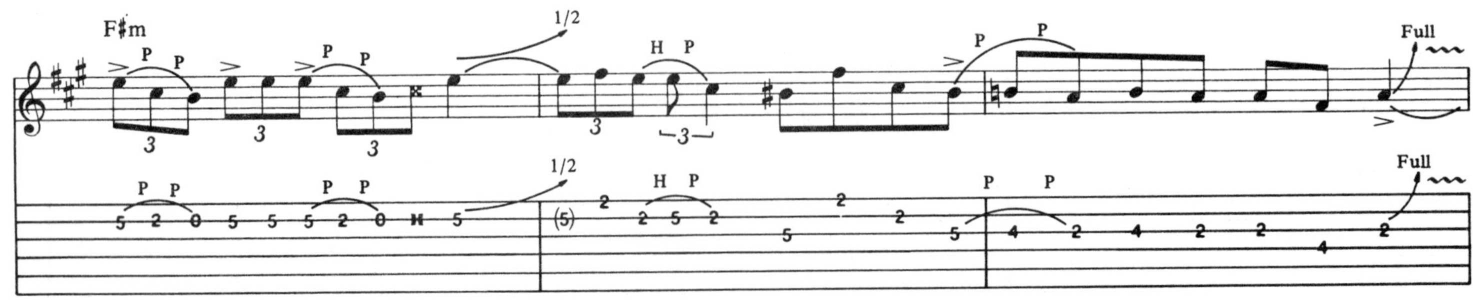

F#m
P P
P P
1/2
H P
P
P
Full
P P
P P
1/2
H P
P
P
Full
5 2 0 5 5 5 2 0 5
(5)
2 5 2
2
5
5
4 2 4 2 2
4
2

D.S. al Coda
*Switch to neck pickup.
129

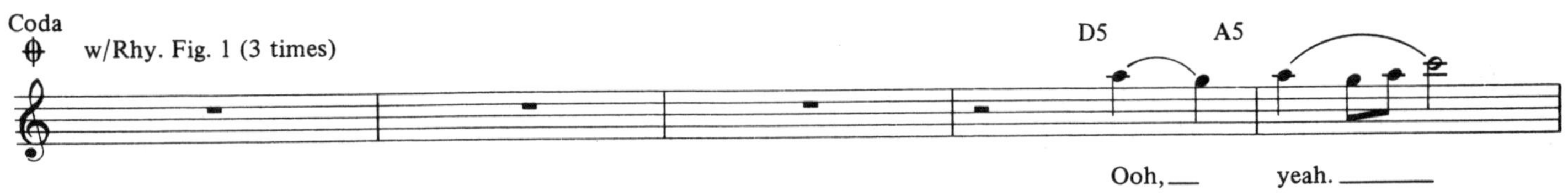

Coda
w/Rhy. Fig. 1 (3 times)
D5   A5
Ooh, ___ yeah. ___

D5   A5   Out-chorus
I've got it bad, ___ got it bad, ___

D5   A5   w/Rhy. Fig. 1 (1st 2 bars only)
___ got it bad, ___ I'm hot for teach - er. ___

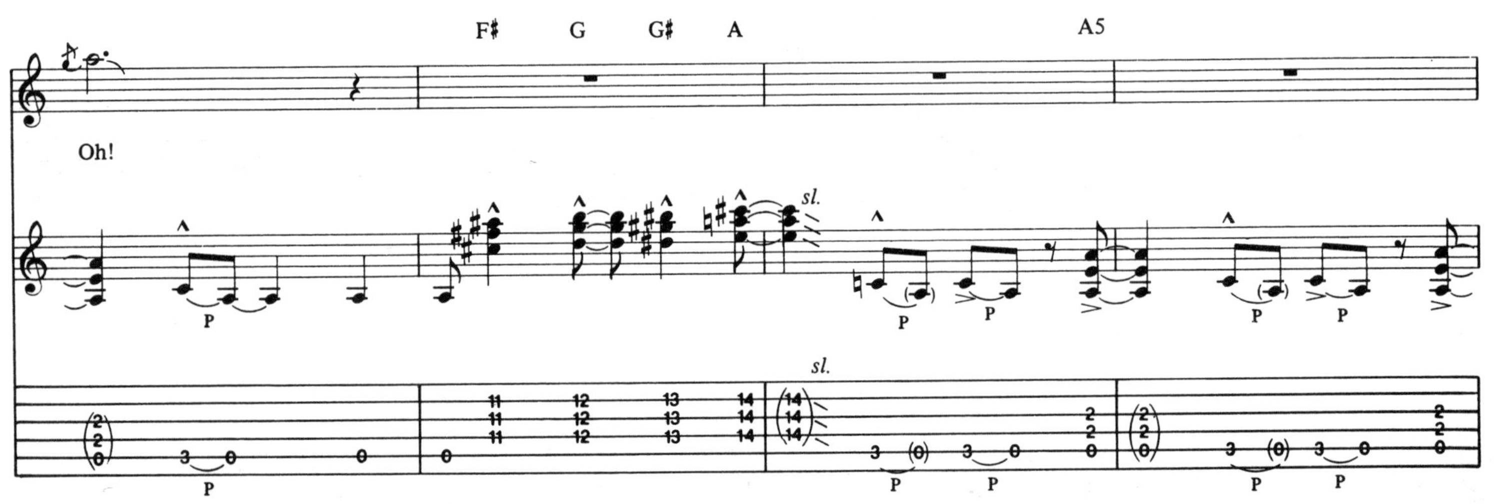

F#   G   G#   A   A5
Oh!
sl.
P   P   P   P
sl.
P   P
11 12 13 14 (14)
11 12 13 14 (14)
11 12 13 14 (14)
(2)   2   (2)   2
(2)   2   (2)   2
(0)   3 (0) 3 0   0   (0) 3 0   0
P

F#   G   G#   A   A5
Oh, oh! ___ Oh, yes ___ I'm hot! ___ Wow. ___
sl.
P   P   P   P
sl.
P   P
11 12 13 14 (14)
11 12 13 14 (14)
11 12 13 14 (14)
2   (2)   2
2   (2)   2
(0)   3 0 3 0   (0)   3 (0) 3 0   0
P   P   P   P

F# G G# A F# G G# A F# G G# A
Free time
N.C.
Oh my God!
G5
trem. pick
P.M.
sl.
w/echo
pick slides
(steady gliss.)
trem. bar
Whoo!
Full
1½
1½
** Echoplex on
*Trem. pick while bending.
**Echo repeats plus feedback control of
tape echo unit (for modulating effect).
A
C D A
trem. pick
* (steady gliss.)
*Trem. pick while sliding chord form.

WHY CAN'T THIS BE LOVE

Words and Music by
Edward Van Halen, Sammy Hagar,
Michael Anthony and Alex Van Halen

F   G   E5 w/Fill 2   D5
up in-side___ ev-'ry time___ we touch.___   Hey,___ I don't know,___   oh___ tell me___
P H P   trem. bar
P   H   P   P   H H   P H   H P

A5   F5   *sl. G(type 2)   Esus4   E5
where   to   be-gin___   'cause I nev-er, ev-er   felt   so___ much.___   Hey!
H   H   P   P   P

Pre-chorus   ⑤7fr.10fr.
Bb5   E G FVIII   *sl.   Ebsus2 w/Fill 3
sl.   sl.   sl.   sl.
And I can't re-call___   an-y love___ at all.___   Ah   ba-by, this blows 'em all___ a-way.___
(end of Riff A)
P   P   P   H

Fill 2   E5   1 A.H. (15ma)   D5
trem. bar   trem. bar   trem. bar
1 A.H.
A.H. pitch: A

Fill 3   —3—   F5
sl.   H
sl.

Chorus
It's got what it takes, so tell me why can't this be love? Straight from my heart, oh, tell me why can't this be love? I tell my-self hey, on-ly fools rush in, on-ly time will tell if we stand the test of time. All I know, you got to run to win, and I'll be damned if I get hung up on the line.

Esus4
E
Pre-chorus
Bb5
sl.
Bbsus4 FVIII
w/Fill 4
Eb
Hey!
No, I can't re-call
an-y-thing at all.
FVIII
GX
Chorus
C
Am7
Ah ba-by, this blows 'em all a-way.
Woo!
It's got what it takes,
H
P
P H P H
sim.
G2(type 2) F5VIII
G5V
C
G(type 2) Am7
so tell me why can't this be love?
You want it straight from the heart,
P
sl.
sl.
w/Fill 5
F
G
N.C.
Asus2
oh, tell me why can't this be love?
P
P
P P
Fill 4
Eb
sl.
sl.
sl.
sl.
sl.
sl.
Fill 5 Am7
F
G
Asus2
sl.
P P
sl.
P P

Bridge
N.C.
Da doo da doo da doo da   da   da doo   da doo da doo   da_   da doo da   da doo   da doo da doo   da   da doo   da doo da doo   da_
Gtr. II
P.M.
P.M.
Gtr. I
Guitar solo
N.C.
da_ doo.
trem. bar
trem. bar

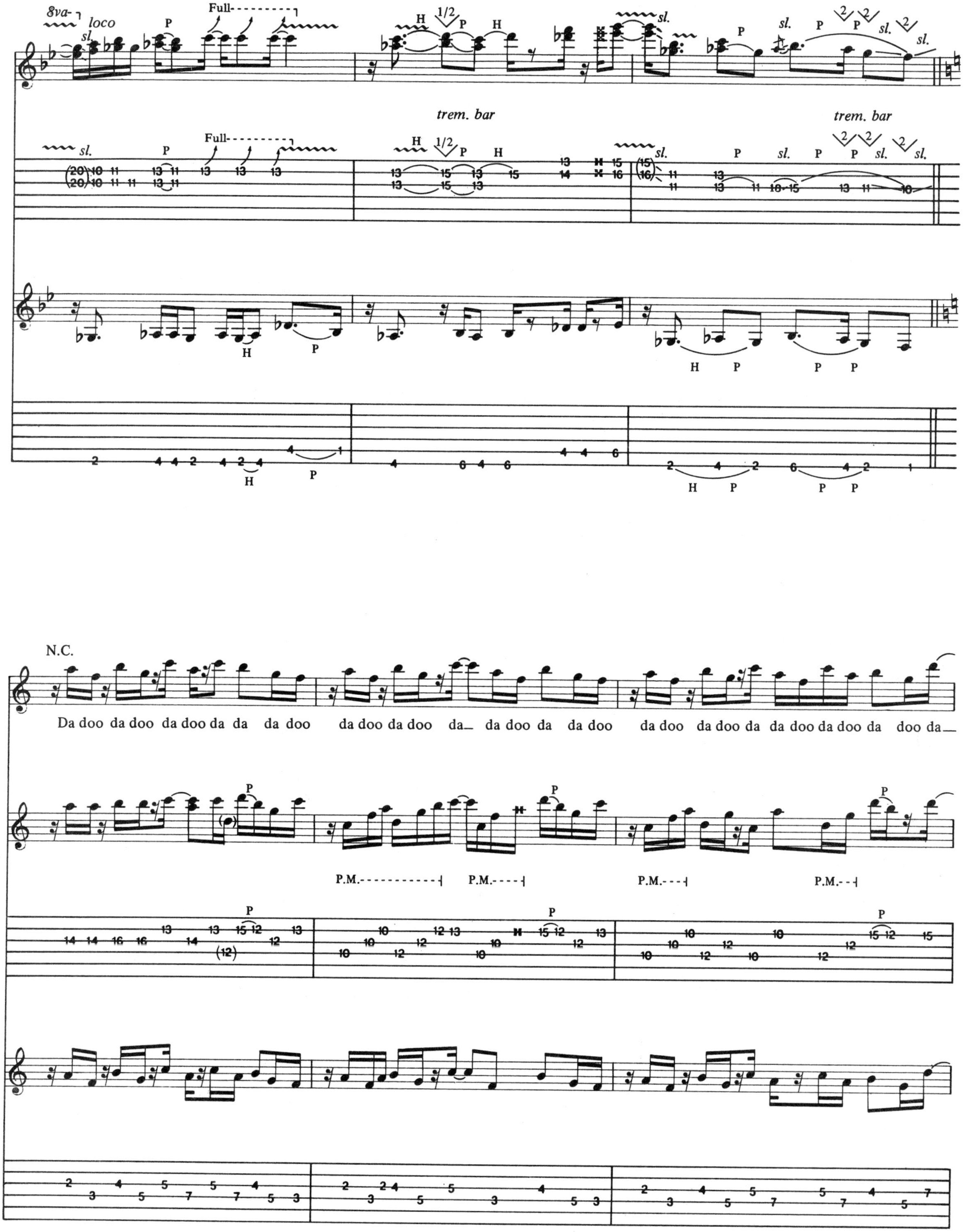

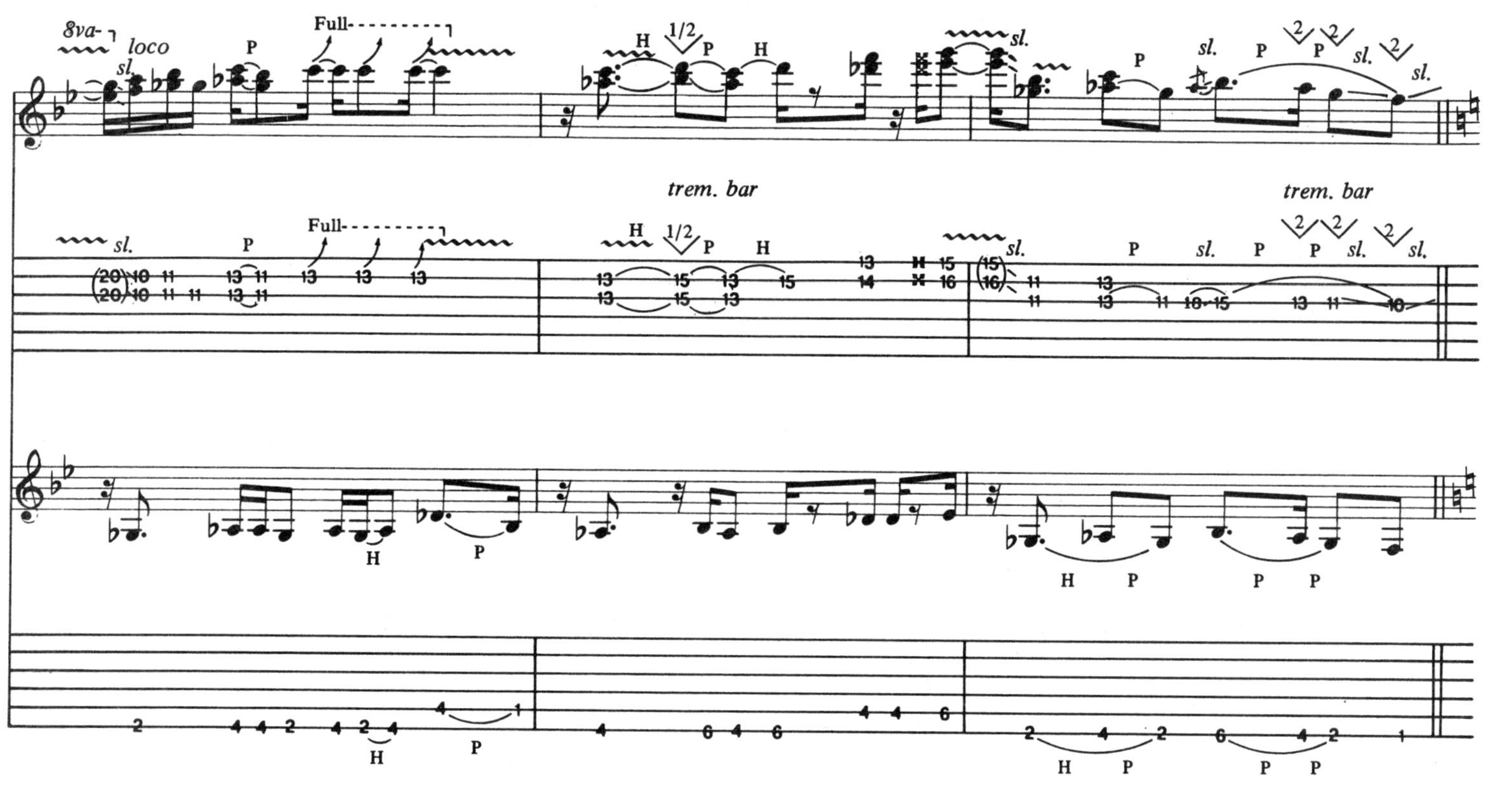

Da doo da doo da doo da da da doo   da doo da doo da_ da doo da da doo   da doo da doo da da doo da doo da doo da_

Chorus
C
G(type 2) Am7
w/Fill 6
da doo.
Woo!
It's got what it takes,
so tell me why
P P sl.
P P sl.
(15) 13 12 10
P
sl.
H P H
sim.
P
(7) 5 4
7
2 3 2 3
(3) 2 3 2 3 3 2 3
(3) 2 3 2 3 2 3 5 3
sl.
H P H
G5
C
Am7
G(type 2) F5
G5
sl. C
can't this be love?
Straight from the heart,
tell me why
can't this be love?
H
P
P H
P
(3) 2 3 2 3 2 3 5 3
(3) 2 3 2 3 3
(3) 2 3
(3) 2 3 2 3 2 3
5 3
(3) 2 3 2 3 2 3 5 3
H
P
P H
P
A.H.
G5
C
Fill 6
A.H.
(5)
5
5
5 4 5
(5)
7
5
5
5
6
5
3
A.H. pitch: E

Am7
F
G
C
pick sl.
F
G
C
Ba - by, why can't this be love? Got to know why can't this be love?
pick sl.
F
G
C
pick sl.
F
G
I wan-na know why can't this be love?
Begin fade
N.C.
Gtr. II
sl.
Fade out
sl. sl. sl. sl.
sl.
sl. sl. sl. sl.
Gtr. I

BEST OF BOTH WORLDS

Words and Music by
Edward Van Halen, Sammy Hagar,
Michael Anthony and Alex Van Halen

1st Verse
*A/C#   G/A   D/F#   A   D7sus4   D/A   A
I don't know what I been livin' on, but it's not enough to fill me up.
sl. mf
sl.   sl.   P
*Bass plays A pedal throughout verse sections.
sl.

A/C#   G/A   D/A   A   D7sus4   D/A
I need more than just-a words can say, I need ev'rything this life can give me. Hey, hey,
sl.
sl.   sl.   P   sl.   6½   P trem.   sl. P bar 6½

D/F#   G   D/F#   G   D/F#   G   A5   D/F#   G   D/F#   Asus2
yeah!   'Cause sometimes it's not enough!   Ow!
f   T   T   T   T   P   Full   Full

2nd Verse
A/C#   G/A   D/F#   A   A/C#   D7sus4   D/A   A
Come on, baby, close your eyes, let go. This can be ev'rything we dreamed, ah.
sl. mf
sl.   sl.   P.M.P
sl.

A/C# G/A D/F# A A/C# D7sus4 Gsus4 G Gsus4 G F
It's not work that makes it work, oh, no, let the mag-ic do the work for you. 'Cause hon-ey,
sl. sl. sl. P
H
Pre-chorus
w/Fill 1
Fsus2 C/E Esus4 E Esus4 E Bsus4 B D
now, some-thing reached out and touched me. Now I know that
(Both gtrs.)
Let ring
sl. sl. sl.
sl. sl.
w/Fill 2 Chorus w/Rhy. Fill 1 (2nd time only)
Dsus2 F D/F# G D/F# G D/F# G A5 D/F# G D/F#
all I want... I want the best of both worlds. And hon-ey, I know what it's worth.
cresc. f
Fill 1
Gtr. II
Fill 2
Gtr. II
pick slides
Rhy. Fill 1
Gtr. I D/F# G D/F# G A5
Full Full
Full Full

If we could have the best of both worlds, we'd have a lit-tle bit of

heav-en right here on earth, oo! Woo! Well, there's a pic-ture in a gal-ler-y, a
heav-en right here on earth,

fall-en an-gel, look a lot like you. We for-get where we come from some-times.

I had a dream it was, uh, real-ly you. Some-thing reached out and touched me.

D.S. al Coda
Bsus4   B   D   w/Fill 3   F(maj7)
Now I know,— oh, all I want.... I want the
(Both gtrs.)
sl.
Coda
w/Fill 4   Csus2   A5
yeah!
Gtr. I
Guitar solo
Gtr. I (rhy. gtr.)
Gtr. II (lead gtr.)
E5 B B5   E5 B B5   G C   G G5   D   A5   D   A B
⑥3fr.
Full   sl.   sl. Full   sl.   Full   H   **1/2   P H P P   sl. P P   P Full P
f
grad. release bar   trem. bar   trem. bar **1/2
Full   sl.   sl. sl. Full   sl.   Full   H
*Play ⑥ only (muted).   **Pull up 1/2 step.
E5 B   E5   B   G   C G   C G   C
⑥3fr.
Full   P   sl.   T   P   1/2 Full   T P   H   Full †1½   *H   T   sl. P M.   P.M. T P   Full
hold bend   hold bend   trem. bar   Full †1½
†Pull up on bar in addition to bending.
G   C   D5   E5   A5 II
P H   T   sl. P Full P   Full   P H   Full   H   Full   T P   T   sl.
hold bend   trem. bar   sl.
2/4
Fill 3
Gtr. II
pick slide
Fill 4
Gtr. II
A.H.   1/2   1   3½   2½
f   trem. bar
A.H.   1/2   1   3½   2½
A.H. pitch: D

Gtr. I
mf (pick w/fingers)
don't pick
sl.
*A pedal implied (see intro).
Wo!
4th Verse
Uh, you don't have to die and go to heav-en, uh, or hang a-round to be
born a-gain. Just tune in to what this place has got to of-fer, 'cause we may nev-er be here a-

w/Fill 5
Chorus
G A Asus2
D/F# G D/F# G D/F# G A5 D/F# G D/F#
gain!_ Ow! I want the best of both worlds,_and hon-ey, I_ know_ what it's worth.
cresc.
(w/pick)
T T T T T
T T T
G A
D/F# G D/F# G D/F# G A5 D/F# G D/F#
If we could have the best of both worlds,_ a lit-tle heav-en right here on earth._
Full Full
T T T
Full Full
P
A
D/F# G D/F# G D/F# G A5 D/F# G D/F#
_ Come on!_ I want the best of both worlds,_ uh, hon-ey, I know what it's worth!_
Full Full
T T T T T
Full Full
Fill 5
Gtr. II
pick slides
sl.
sl.

We can have the best of both worlds, a lit-tle heav-en right here on earth,
yeah!
Tell me, is it e-nough?
Wow!
Now, will it ev-er be e-nough?
Fill 6
Gtr. II
w/Fill 6

Free time
C5 A5
In time
A
G/A
poco rit. Wo!
poco rit.
mp (pick w/fingers)
D/A G/A D/A G/A D/A A G/A D/A G/A A A7sus2 A G/A
cresc.
mf
D/A G/A D/A G/A D/A A G/A D/A G/A A A7sus2 A G/A
P.M.
Begin fade
D/A G/A D/A G/A D/A A G/A D/A G/A A A7sus2 A(6) G/A*
*A pedal implied
by bass figure.
D/A G/A D/A G/A D/A A G/A D/A G/A A D/A F6/A F#+/A G/A Fade out

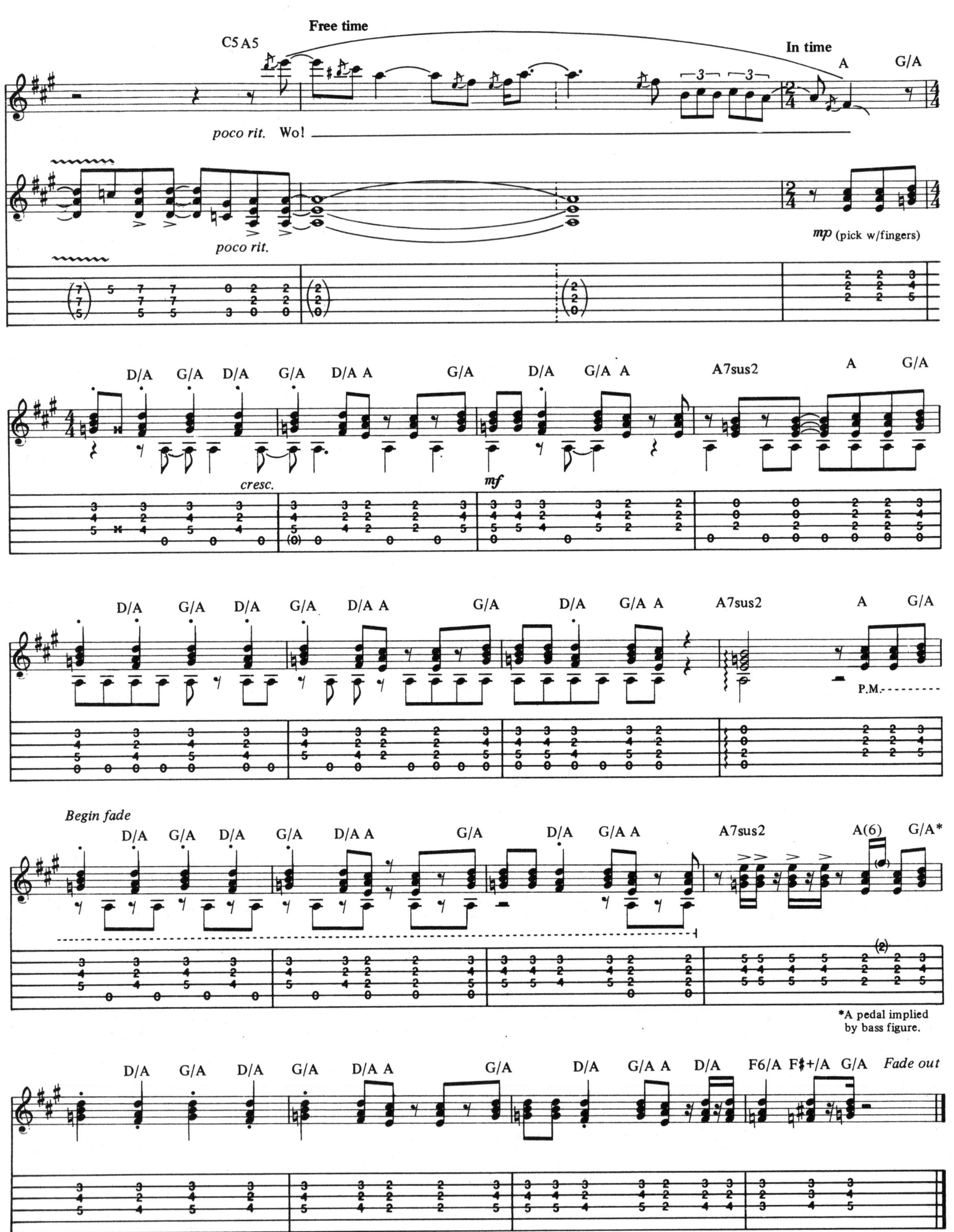

148

"5150"

Words and Music by
Edward Van Halen, Sammy Hagar,
Michael Anthony and Alex Van Halen

Tune down:
⑥ = D♭ ③ = G♭
⑤ = A♭ ② = B♭
④ = D♭ ① = E♭

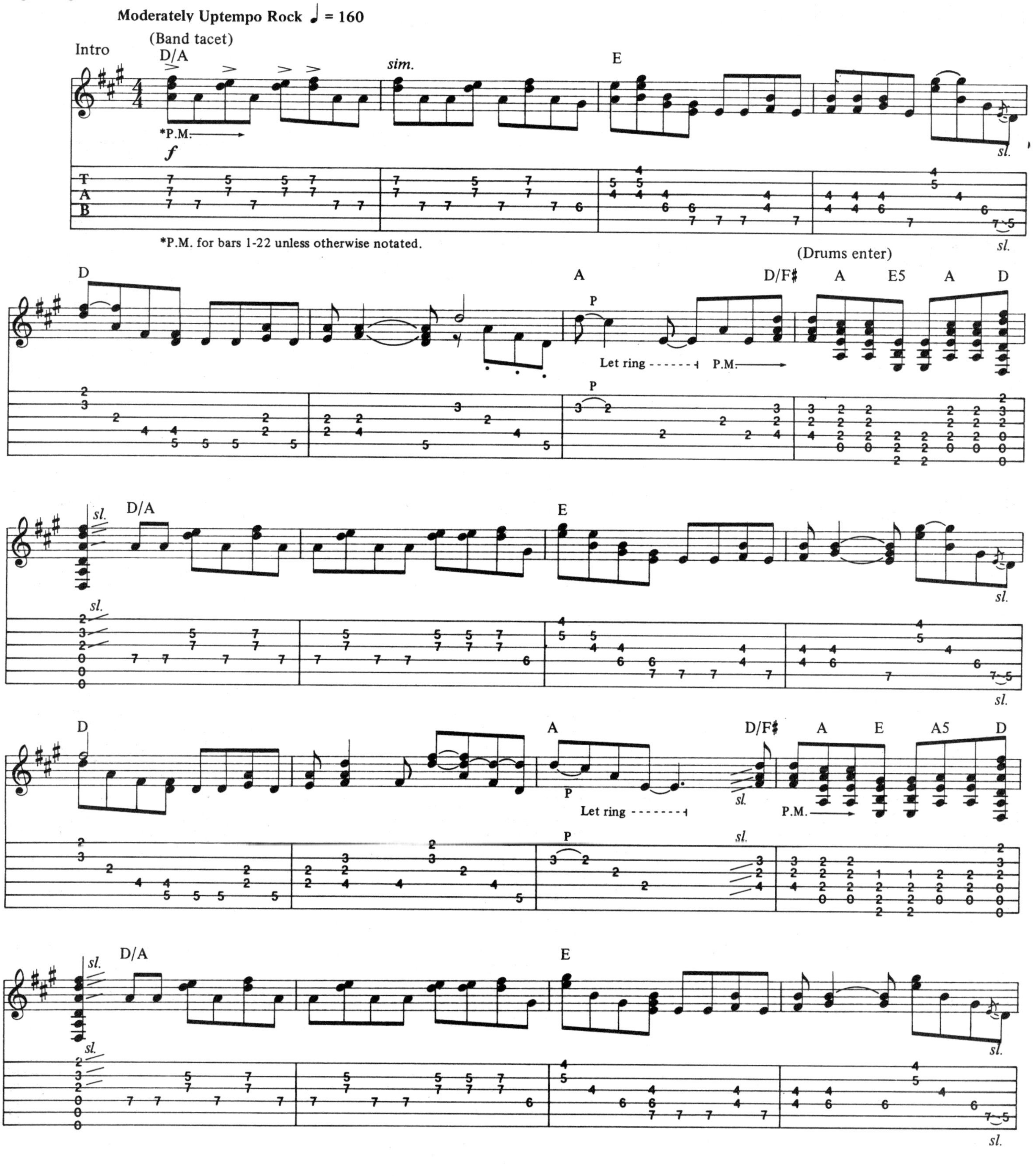

(Bass enters)
Let ring
Half-time feel
1st, 2nd Verses
1. The love line is nev - er straight and nar - row,
2. I feel like a run - ning pol - i - ti - cian.
Oh!

D5
N.C. (G5)
(C5)
1/2
P P P P
1/2
7 7 5
7 7 5
0 0 0 0
0 0 0 0
5 3 0
(4)
P P
0 5 3
P
0
un - less your love____ is tried and true.____
Just tryin' to please____ you all the time.____

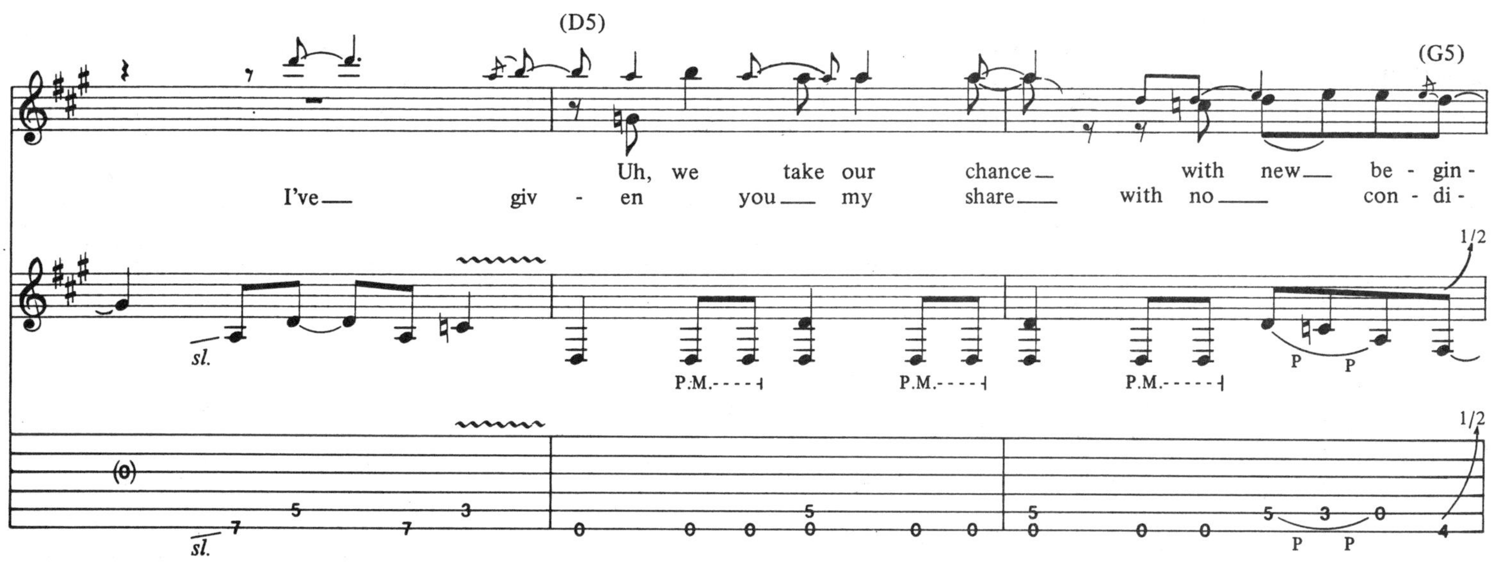

(D5)
(G5)
sl.
P.M.---- P.M.---- P.M.----
1/2
P P
1/2
(0)
sl.
7 5 7 3
0 0 0 5
0 0 0
5 0 0 0
5 3 0
P P
4
sl.
I've____ giv - en you____ my share____ with no____ con - di-
Uh, we take our chance____ with new____ be - gin-

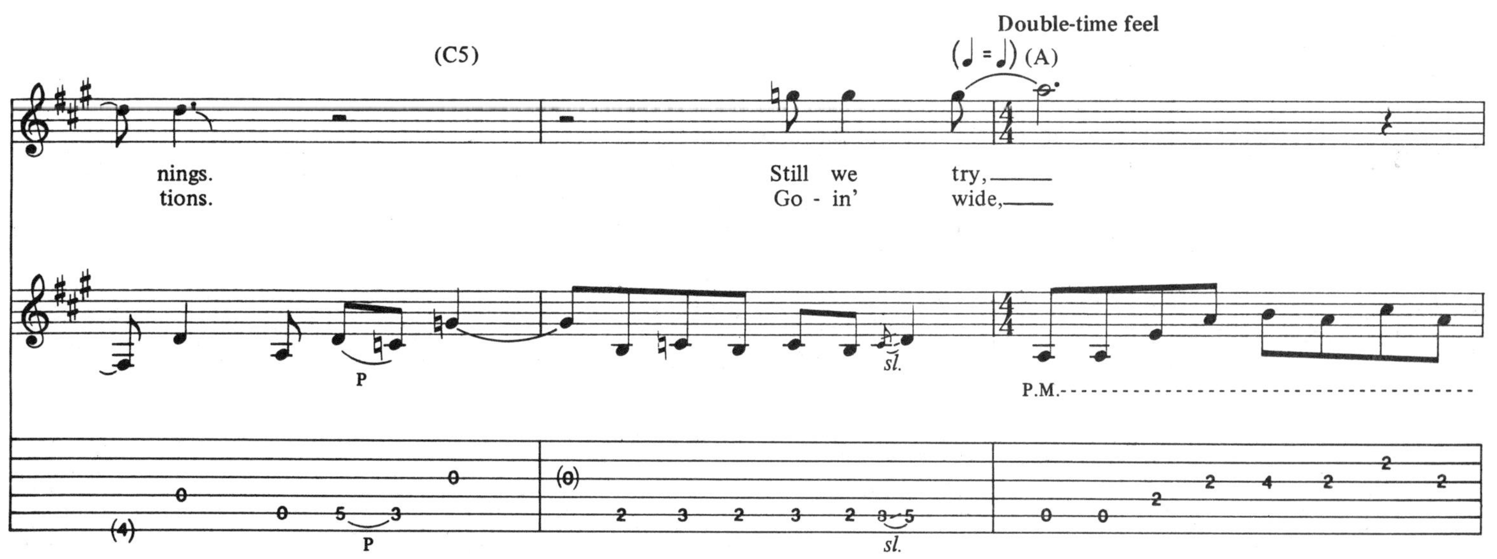

(C5)
Double-time feel
(♩ = ♪) (A)
P
sl.
P.M.-------------------------------
(4)
0
0 5 3
P
0
(0)
2 3 2 3 2 0 5
sl.
0 0
2
2 4 2 2
2
nings. Still we try,____
tions. Go - in' wide,____

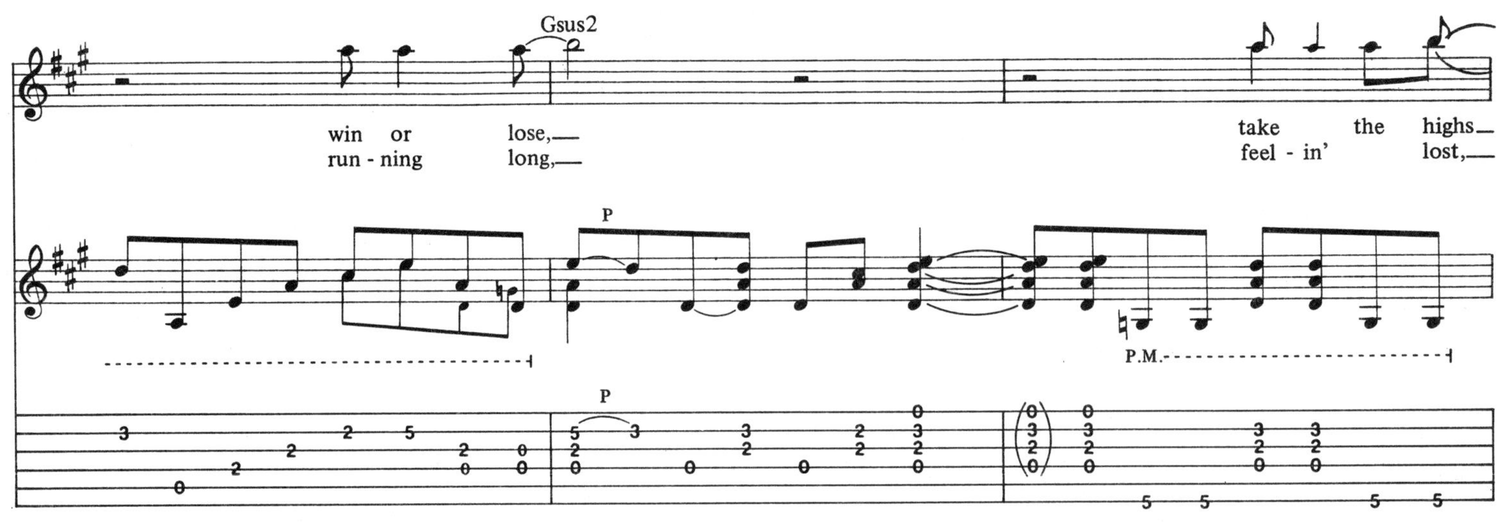

Gsus2
win or lose,
run - ning long,
take the highs
feel - in' lost,
P
P.M.
P

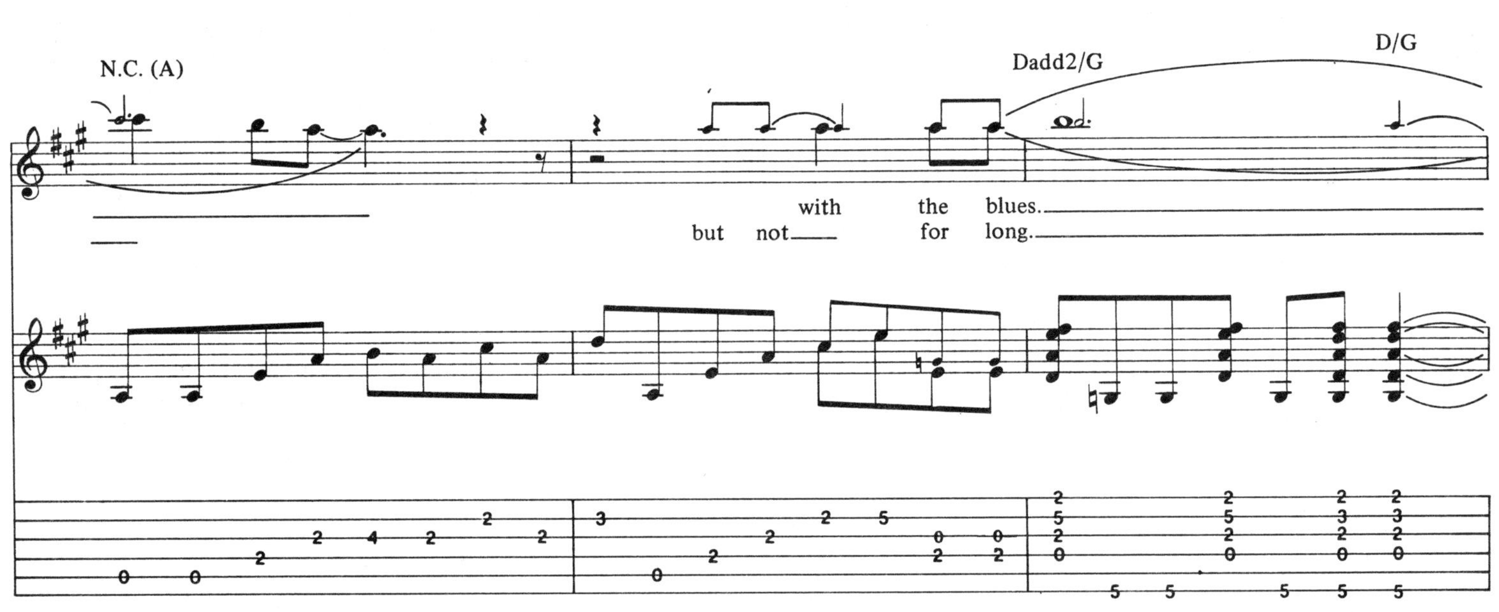

N.C. (A)
Dadd2/G
D/G
with the blues.
but not for long.

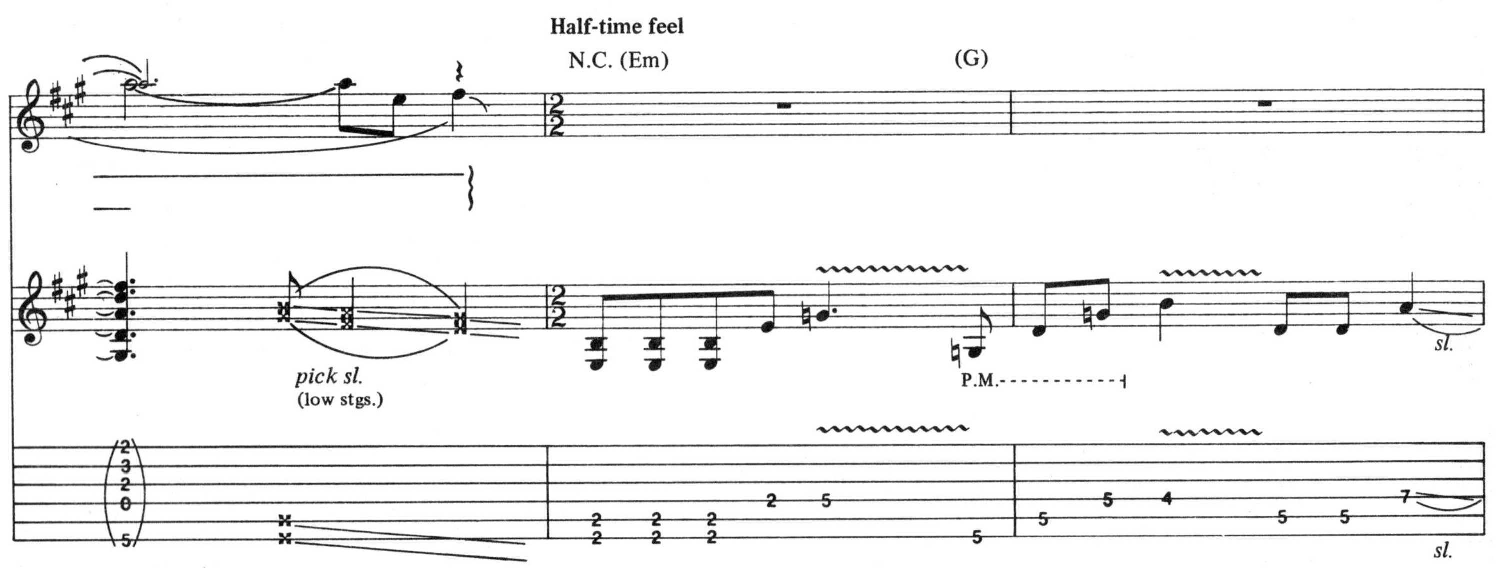

Half-time feel
N.C. (Em)
(G)
pick sl.
(low stgs.)
P.M.
sl.
sl.

(F)
(A)
(C5)
(Dadd9)
sl.
P.M.
sl.
Let ring
Double-time feel
Chorus
N.C.
D
D/A
E/A
Al - ways one more, you're nev - er
Rhy. Fig. 1
sl.
D/A
sat - is - fied, nev - er one for all with you
A.H.
*Sing A 3rd time only.
A.H.
pitch: E
G
A
it's on - ly one for me.
(1.) Oh,
(2.3.) So,
why
P.M.
Let ring
sl.
P
P
sl.
sl.

Repeat Rhy. Fig. 1

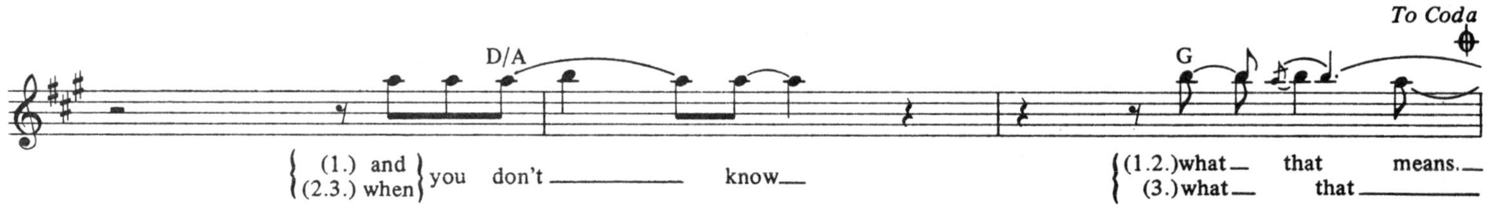

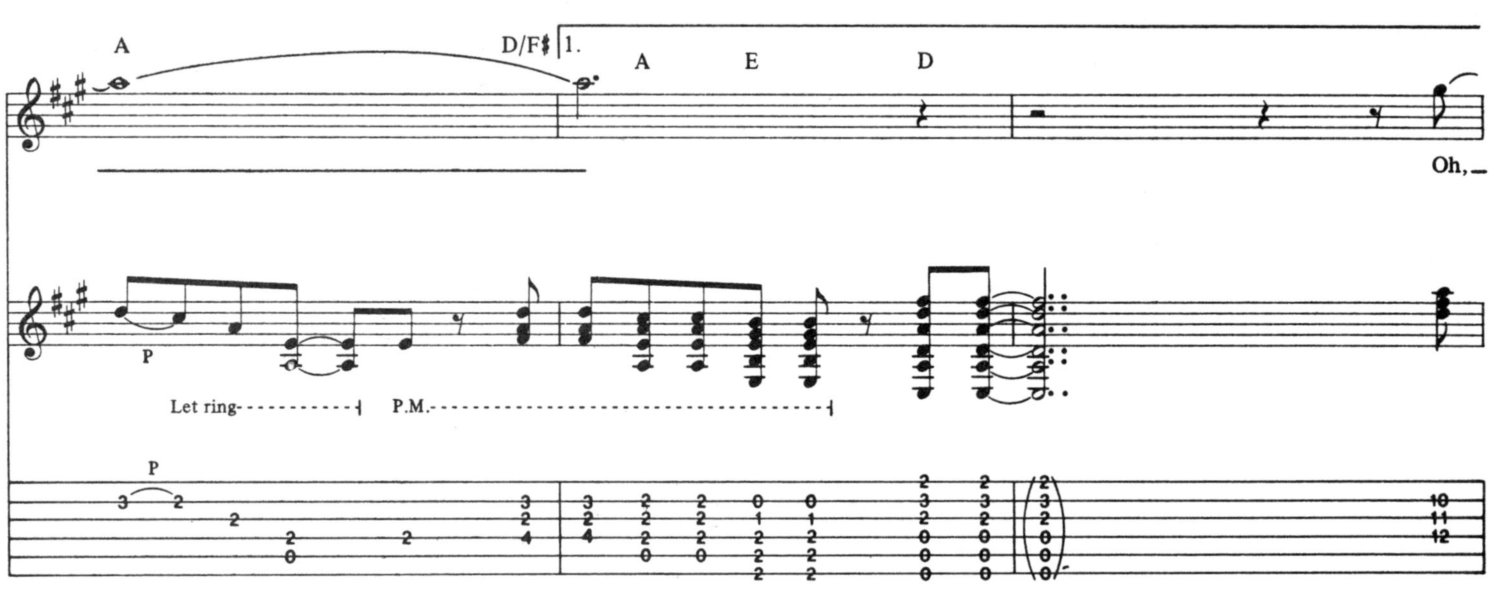

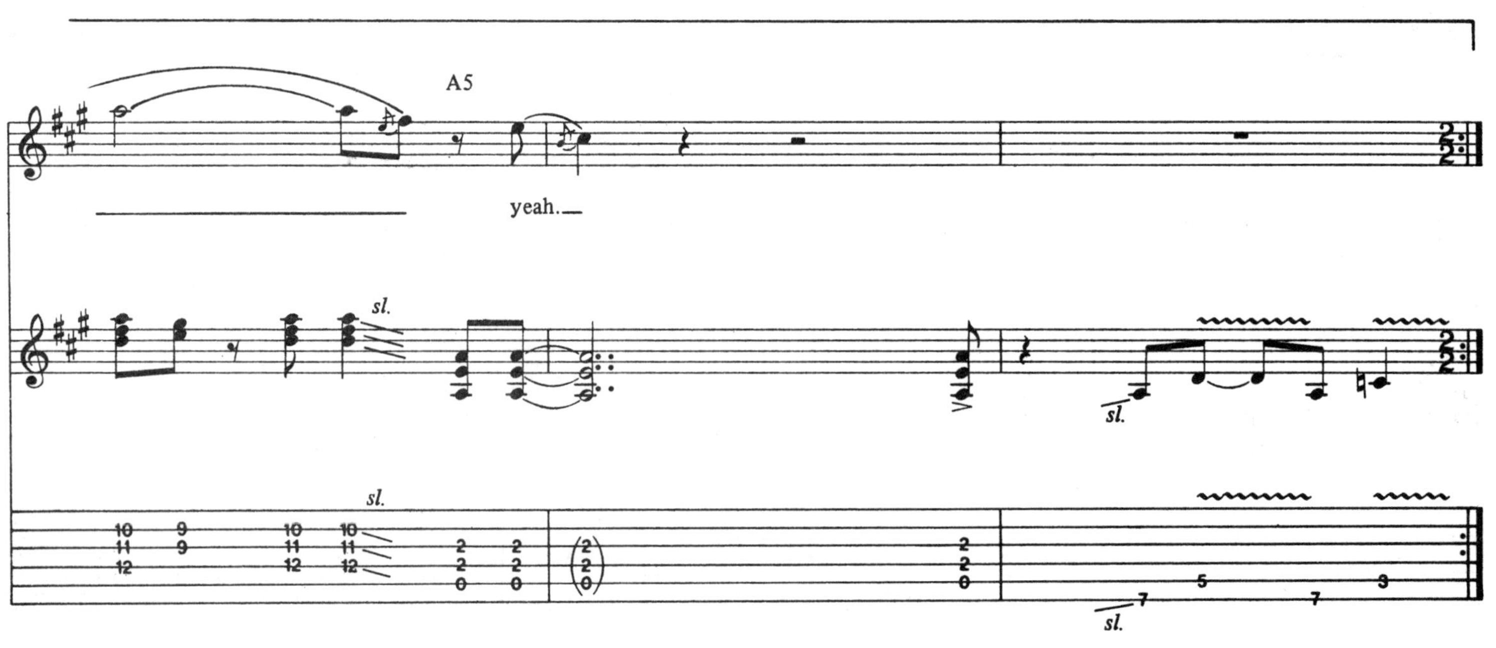

2.
A   E   D5
Whoa,
Gtr. II
sl.
Full
Full
9   11   9   11   11   (11)   11
sl.
Gtr. I
3 2 2 0 0
2 2 2 1 1
4 2 2 2 2
0 0 2 2
2 2
0 0 (0) 0 0
2 2 0 0
2 2 0 0
A
yeah.
Full
1½
3½
Full
1½
trem. bar
3½
16   17 19 19   (19)
16   14 16
sl.
0   (0)
(mid stgs.)
Volume
0 0 0 0 0
0 0 0 0 0
2 2 (2) 2
2 2 2 2
2 0 (2) 0   2 0

155

Guitar solo

*Push string against pick-up pole piece.

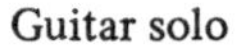

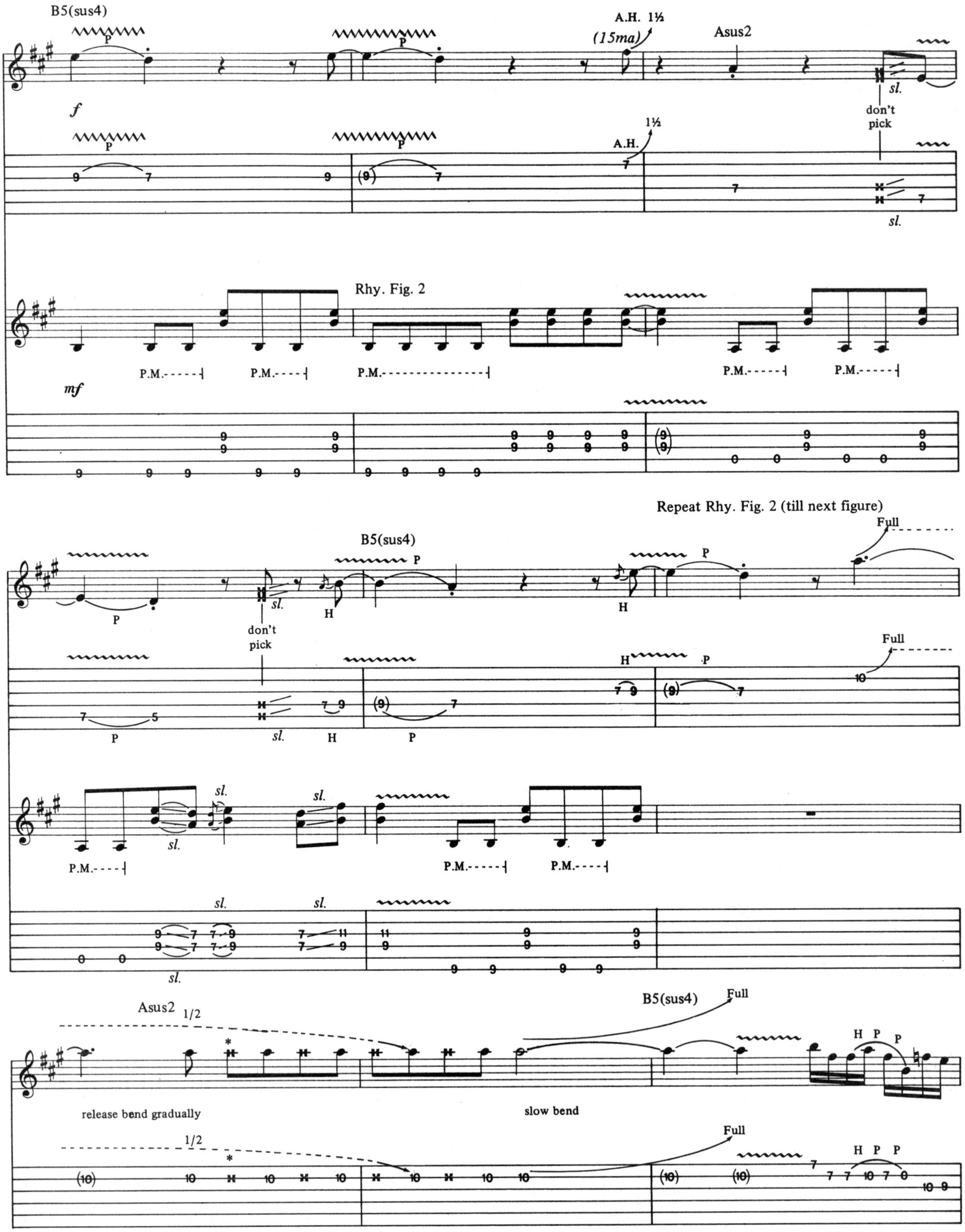

Asus2
B5(sus4)
Asus2
B5(sus4)
Asus2
A.H.
(8va)
1/2
steady
gliss.
A.H.
pitch: C#
Full
Full
Harm.
(8va)
Harm.
(8va)
Full
trem. bar
trem. bar

157

B5(sus4)
sl.
H H P P
Full
Asus2
P
H P
1/2 Full
P
P.M.
B5(sus4)
P.M. P.M. P.M.
P P P P P
6 6
Asus2
P P
3
A.H.
(15ma)
H
sl.
P P
A.H.
sl.
P H
A.H. pitches: C# D#
8va
Asus2 D5 A
Full Full Full Full P *
B5(sus4)
6
(trem. picking)
Full Full Full Full P *
P.M. P.M.
P.M. P.M. P.M.

G/A
F
A
8va
1/2
P
1/2
P
H
P
D/F#
A
E
A
D/A
sl.
1/2
P
1/2
P
H
P
sl.
P.M.
f
(Band tacet)
D/A
E
P.M.
D
sl.
sl.
A
D/F#
A
E
A
D/A
P
Let ring
P.M.
P

E
D
D.S. al Coda
A
Al - ways
Let ring
sl.
P
P
sl.
(Cont. Rhy. Fig. 1)
Coda
Repeat Rhy. Fig. 1 (till fade)
A
D
D/A
E/A
means.
G
A
D/A
I'll meet you half the way.
Whoa,
D
D/A
E/A
yeah!
Begin fade
D/A
G
A
I'll meet you half the way.
Well, I,
D
D/A
E/A
D/A
Fade out
I'll meet you half the way.

CABO WABO

Words and Music by
Edward Van Halen, Sammy Hagar,
Michael Anthony and Alex Van Halen

w/Rhy. Fig. 1
Dsus4
D
E5
(Band in)
A5 D/A E5
A5 D/A
Ah!
(end Rhy. Fig. 1A)
H P.M.-
2nd Verse
w/Rhy. Fig. 1
E5
A5 D/A
E5
There's a sleep-y town___ that's south of the bor-der.___ If you go there once,___ you'll be there twice.___
w/Rhy. Fig. 1A (1st 2 bars only)
A5 D/A
E5
A5 D/A
Lots of pret-ty girls_________ com-in' by the doz-ens. Whoo!
A5 D5 A5 D5 A5
B
Pre-chorus
E5/A
E5
The white sand sure makes a tan look nice.________
We crash on the beach.
whoo,___
Rhy. Fig. 1B
(Whoo,________
(end Rhy. Fig. 1B) Rhy. Fig. 2
H P.M.-
E/G#
A5 B5
N.C.
B
You know__ I wan-na______ make love__ in the sea.___
whoo,___
whoo,___
H H H
H H H

E5/A
E/G#
A5
B
We got-ta try a lit-tle dance, so Ca-bo Wa-bo. It's al-right by me.
whoo, whoo, whoo.)
Chorus
E
D
A
C5
G
Come on! Let me take you down.
(end Rhy. Fig. 2)
Rhy. Fig. 3
sl.
H
sl. sl. H
E
D
Asus2
I will show you all a-round.
(Down in Ca-bo.)
Let me take you down,
P.M.
E
D
A
C5
E
D
Asus2
face down in Ca-bo. Kiss-in' the ground.
(end Rhy. Fig. 3)
sl.
sl.
P.M.

3rd Verse
w/Rhy. Fig. 1
Land's end, you'd have to see it. Ain't no pic-ture ev-er say it right.
w/Rhy. Fig. 1A (1st 2 bars only)
No, whoa. Walk-in' the streets do-ing that ole Ca-bo Wa-bo. Ha!
w/Rhy. Fig. 1B
Place comes to life ev-'ry night. No! I wan-na crash on the beach.
Pre-chorus
w/Rhy. Fig. 2
(Whoo, whoo,
You know I wan-na make love in the sea.
whoo, whoo, whoo,
Yeah. It's al-right there. We don't have to chase it. Fits par-a-dise to a T.
whoo, whoo, whoo.)
Chorus
w/Rhy. Fig. 3
Whoo! Come on! Let me take you down.
w/Rhy. Fill 1
I will show you all a-round.
(Resume Rhy. Fig. 3)
(Down in Ca-bo.)
w/Rhy. Fill 2
Let me take you down,
(Resume Rhy. Fig. 3)
face down in Ca-bo. Kiss-in' the ground.
Rhy. Fill 1
Rhy. Fill 2
Harm. (8va)
Harm.

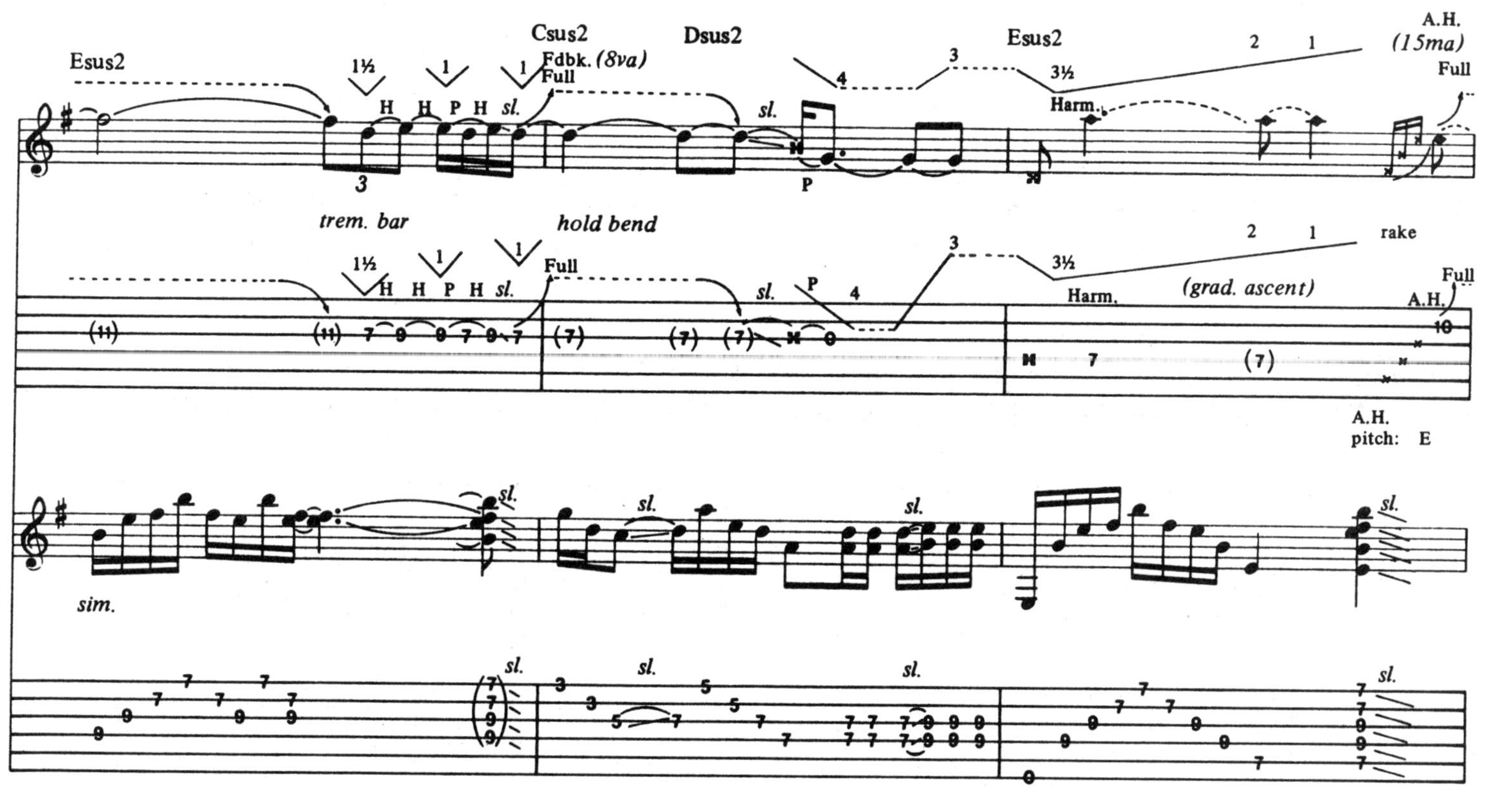
Guitar solo
B5
Esus2
Dsus2
Gtr. I
8va
Full
loco
Full
1½
w/Wah (as filter and
boost) and echo. Harmonizer
brought in sparingly.
hold bend
trem. bar
Full
1½
Full
Gtr. II (12-stg.elec.)
sl.
let ring
let ring
let ring
sl.
sl.
Esus2
Csus2
Dsus2
Esus2
A.H.
(15ma)
1½
1
1
Fdbk. (8va)
Full
3
3½
2
1
Full
H H P H sl.
Harm.
3
trem. bar
hold bend
P
1½
1
1
Full
3
3½
2
1
rake
H H P H sl.
Harm.
(grad. ascent)
Full
A.H.
A.H.
pitch: E
sim.
sl.
sl.
sl.
sl.
sl.
sl.
sl.
sl.

Dsus2
Esus2
Gsus2   Asus2
Dsus2
Esus2
A.H.
Csus2
Esus2
Dsus2
8va
trem. bar
loco
P H
*Articulated w/trem. bar
(don't pick).
A.H. hold bend
trem. bar
(trem. pick)
Full
sl.

Esus2
8va
Full
sl.
Full
Gsus2 Asus2 Fsus2 Gsus2 Am7 D Bm Fmaj7 G
Full
sl.
sl.
Full
22 22-12 14 15 17 19-22 (22) (22) (22)
*
*Sustained w/Fdbk.
sl.
sl.
sl.
sl.
sl.
sl.
sl.
P.M.
sl.
Bridge
Csus2 G/B Csus2 G/B Csus2 G/B Csus2 G/B D Dsus4 Csus2 G5 Csus2 G5 Csus2 G5
sl. sl.
(Both gtrs.)
Wah.
Gsus2 Asus2 Csus2 G/B Csus2 G/B Csus2 G/B Dsus2 D
Hey!
Wah!
let ring
(C) (D) (C) (D) (F#o) (G) (Cmaj7) Gtr. I D
(Band tacet)
Gtr. I
*
Gtr. II
slight P.M.
H P.M.
*Muted stgs. (allow
random harmonics
to sound).
H

w/Rhy. Fig. 1
4th Verse
w/Rhy. Fig. 1A
E5   A5   D/A   E5   A5   D/A   E5
We drink Mes-cal

A5   D/A   E5   Dsus4   D
right from the bot-tle.   Salt shak-er, lit-tle lick a lime,   ah.

w/Rhy. Fig. 1 (1st 2 bars only)
w/Rhy. Fig. 1B
E5 (Band in)   A5   D/A   E5
Throw-in' down, down, try'n' to reach the bot-tom where the gua-ve worm, well, he's

A5   D5   A5   D5 A5   B   Pre-chorus w/Rhy. Fig. 2   E5/A   E/G#
mine, all mine. Ha ha.   Come on, crash on the beach.   You know I wan-na

A5   B5   (Whoo,   N.C.   A   whoo,   E5/A   whoo,
make love in the sea.   Whoo!   Go try a lit-tle dance, whoo,

E/G#   whoo.   A5   B   Whoo,
So Ca-bo Wa-bo.   It's all right by me.   whoo,   whoo.)

Chorus
w/Rhy. Fig. 3   w/Rhy. Fill 1
E   D   A   C5   G   E   Asus2
Let me take you down.   I will show you all a-

(Resume Rhy. Fig. 3)   E   D   A   C5   G
round.   Let me take you down,   face down in Ca-

(Down in Ca-bo.)   w/Rhy. Fill 3
E   D   Asus2   B5
bo.   Kiss-in' the ground.

B5
Gtr. II (12-stg. elec.)
Rhy. Fill 3

Outro
Esus2   Dsus2   Esus2   Csus2   Dsus2
Whoo. C'-mon.   Face
let ring- - - - - - - - - - - - - - - sim.
sl.

Esus2   Dsus2   Asus2   Gsus2   Asus2
down,   down in Ca-bo.   Take me down,
(Face   down.)
sl.

Esus2   Dsus2   Esus2   Csus2   Dsus2
down in Ca-bo.   Uh!   Face
(Take me down.)
sl.

Esus2   Dsus2   Asus2   Gsus2   Asus2
down,   down in Ca-bo.   Do-in' the Ca-bo Wa-bo.   Ow!   Take me down,
(Face   down.)
sl.

Esus2
Dsus2
Esus2
Csus2
Dsus2
down in Ca - bo.
Whoo!
Come on,
get it, get it!
(Take me down.)
sl.
H
sl.
sl.
sl.
H
Esus2
Dsus2
Asus2
Gsus2
Asus2
Oh!
Ah - ha!
Whoo-hoo!
Ow!
C' - mon!
sl.
sl.
sl.
sl.
sl.
sl.
Begin fade
Esus2
Dsus2
Esus2
sl.
sl.
sl.
sl.
sl.
Csus2
Dsus2
Esus2
Dsus2
sl.
sl.
sl.
sl.
sl.
sl;
Asus2
Gsus2
Asus2
Fade out
sl.
sl.
sl.
sl.
sl.

FINISH WHAT YA STARTED

171

A5
Wow__ wow__ wow__

D5/E E5(type 2)   E D5/E   E5(type 2)   G5/A   A5   G5/A   A5   D5/E
⑥ open
unh!

E5(type 2)   D5/E   E5(type 2)   G5/A   A5   G5/A   A5   D5/E

1st Verse
Rhy. Fig. 1
E5   D5/E   E5(type 2)   G/A   A   G/A
Well, if you wan-na see oth-er guys,___ ba-by, I could let it___

(end Rhy. Fig. 1) w/Rhy. Fig. 1 (1st 3 bars only)
A   D5/E   E5   D5/E E5(type 2)   G/A   A   G/A
slide.
You wan-na lov-er, you want a friend. Ma-ma, I can be both
H H   H H   H H
Pre-chorus
⑤open 2fr. ⑥3fr.
A   A B G B   A5 B5 B(type 2)   A5 B5 G/A
of them. I got the tools to sat-is-fy.
H H   H H
sl.
A   C#m   D#m C#m   B(type 2) C#m
Just walk a-way if I fall shy at all.
sl.
H H   H H
sl.
D   Chorus
E5
Ah.   Come on, ba-by, fin-ish what you start-ed,
1/2   1/2
sl.   H H   H H
sl.
173

I'm in-com-plete.___ Uh! That ain't no way to treat the bro-ken-heart-ed.
I need some sym-pa-thy.___ Well, I like to look at the long___
___ run,___ I like to take each___ step one___ by one.___
Right on time,___ you will ar-rive___ by keep-in' the dream___ a-live.___

Pre-chorus
It's a - live and it's kick - in' in - side of me.
So come on ba - by, please.
Chorus
Come on, ba - by, fin - ish what you start - ed. Oh! I'm in - com - plete.
Unh. That ain't no way to treat the bro - ken - heart - ed. Ow! Come on and fin -

Guitar solo
F#
G5(type 2)
D5
A
ish me.
Ba - by, come on.
sl.
sl.
F#
G5(type 2)
D5
F#
Come on, ba - by!
You say
yeah.
sl.
sl.
sl.
G5(type 2)
D5
A
F#
G5
D5
Ba - by, come on.
Ba - by, ba - by, ba - by, ba - by, ba - by, ba-!
Full
Full
B5
B
E5
yeah!
rake
P
1/2
P
1/4
sl.
3
*Lay back time slightly for one bar.
sl.
H H

176

A5
⑥open ⑥3fr.
E   G 1/2   E5(type 2)
Unh!
Now, come on, — ba-by.
Please.
H H
H H
H H
H H
⑥12fr.
E
A5
w/Rhy. Fill 1
Oh,   ba - by,   come on.
1/4
1/2
1/4
1/2
H H
H H
Chorus
E5
A5
G5/A
Come on,   ba - by, fin - ish what — you start - ed.
Ah.
H H
sl.   H
H H
Rhy. Fill 1
Gtr. II

That ain't no way to treat the bro - ken - heart - ed.
Nnn,
wow wow ah.
Come on ba - by, fin - ish what you start - ed.
Wooh!
Gim-me! Unh! That ain't no way to treat the
bro - ken - heart - ed.
Mm, mm, (Ba - by, come on.)

Outro
E5(type 2)
E7
D5/E
E5(type 2)
G5/A
A5
G5/A
G/A
ah.
Take each step, ba - by, one ____ by one.
H H
H H
6 open
A
G5
E
D5/E
E5(type 2)
D5/E
E5(type 2)
D5/E
G5/A
(Ba - by, come on.) ____
Yeah. ____
C' - mon.
1/4
1/4
A5
G/A
A
G/A
E5(type 2)
w/Rhy. Fill 2
(Ba-by, come on.) ____ I got the tools, ____ I'll sat - is - fy. ________
H H
H H
H H
H H
Rhy. Fill 2
Gtr. II
sl.
sl.
sl.
sl.
sl.
sl.
sl.
sl.

A
G5/A A5
A
6 3fr.
G 1/2
6 open
E
w/Rhy. Fill 3
C'-mon ba-by. (Ba-by, come on.)
Wow
sl.
sl.
G/A A
Asus4 E5 (type 2)
wow.
Yeah.
(Ba-by, come on.)
H
sl.
H
sl.
w/Rhy. Fill 4
Begin fade
5 open
A A A5 G5/A
(Ba-by, come on.)
1/4
1/4
sl.
Rhy. Fill 3
Gtr. II
sl. sl. sl. sl.
Rhy. Fill 4
Gtr. II
sl. sl. sl. sl.

w/Rhy. Fill 5
(Ba - by, come on.)
So, c' - mon, ba - by.
(Ba - by, come on.)
A
G/A A
w/Rhy. Fill 1(2nd half)
w/Rhy. Fill 4
So, c' - mon, ba - by.
(Ba - by, come on.)
Shout!
A
G/A A
E
G
open 3fr.
Fade out
E5(type 2)
Now, come on.
(Ba - by, come on.)
Now, come on.
Now, come on.
(Ba - by, come on.)
Rhy. Fill 5
Gtr. II
trem. pick

316

Music by Edward Van Halen, Alex Van Halen,
Michael Anthony and Sammy Hagar

*Tapped harmonics.

POUNDCAKE

Words and Music by
Edward Van Halen, Alex Van Halen,
Michael Anthony and Sammy Hagar

Harm.
(8va)
E5
Dsus2/A
C/G
Aadd2
N.C.
1st Verse
E5
N.C.
Yeah!_ She's got-ta have soul,______
E5
N.C.
or it won't feel___ right.______
Well, just
E5
N.C.
play___ clean_ an' sim-ple, wrapped up nice 'n' tight.
An'
A.H.
(15ma)
Harm.
(8va)
Harm.
(8va)
A.H. pitch: G#
P.M.
Harm.
semi-
harm.
(8va)
Harm. pitches: G# E
*Lightly touch stg. slightly behind 3rd fret,
sounding both B & D harmonics.

Chorus
E5
D5 D6/9(no 3rd)
w/elec. drill
Aadd9/C#
home grown, an' down home, that makes a wom-an, uh!
sl.
sl.
E5
D5 D6/9(no 3rd)
Cook - in' up that old time, long lost rec - i - pe
Harm.
(15ma)
sl.
sl.
Add9/C#
N.C.
2nd Verse
N.C.(E5)
for me! Woo! It's get - tin' hard to find,
Harm.
(8va)
*1 1/2
1/2 1
pick slide
trem. bar
trem. bar
P.M.
P.M.
Harm.
(8va)
P H P H P H
H P H P H P
sl.
*Depress bar before striking note..Lightly touch stg. at 5fr. w/o picking to sound harmonic.
E5
N.C.
guess it ain't hip e - nough now. You take an
Harm.
(8va)
P.M.
P.M.
Harm.

(A5)
ave - rage   guy, _____
he can't i - den - ti - fy.
Harm.
(8va)
P.M.
Harm.
(E5)
Uh!   An' there's a short   sup - ply, _____
of the fine, _____
Harm.
(8va)
P.M.
semi-
harm.
Harm.
E5   N.C.
Pre-chorus
B
fine ___ stuff.
Let me get on! Let me get on! ___ Let me get on some of that.
Harm.
(8va)
Harm.
(8va)
P.M.
Harm.
Harm.
sl. sl.
sl. sl.
C5 N.C.(G5) D5 A5   N.C.   B
C5   G5   Dsus4 D   N.C.
Shake it up!   Bake it up   nice! _ Mm!
Let me get on! _
P.M.

B
C5 G5 D5 A5 N.C. B
Let me get on! Let me get on all that! I sure love___ my ba-by's pound-cake.
P.M.------
sl.
sl.
C
Chorus
E5 D6/9(no 3rd)
Home___ grown_ an' down_____ home, oo, yeah, that's a
P.M. P.M.
don't pick
sl.
Aadd9/C# N.C. E5
wom-an,___ uh. Still cook-in' with an old time_
Harm.------
(8va)
Harm.
P
sl.
D5 D6/9(no 3rd) Aadd9/C# N.C.
long lost rec - i - pe.___ Lem-me get on___ some of that!_
Harm.
(8va)
1½ 2½ 2½
H P trem. bar
(grad. descent)
Harm.
H P 1½ 2½ 2½
sl.

Bridge
(Bass plays E pedal
A B G A E E D E D E G
Uh, a, huh, huh!
(A pedal
A B G A E
Uh, a, huh, huh!
Rhy. Fig. 1
sl.
w/slide
w/o slide
w/slide
D C
(E pedal sim.)
A B G A E E D E D E G
Yeah! I want some-a that... Uh, a, huh, huh! Gim-me some-a that...
(end Rhy. Fig. 1)
sl.
w/slide
w/o slide
w/slide
(A pedal
A E G A
(B pedal)
B
E/G#
B
Guitar solo
N.C.(F#5)
Uh, a, huh, huh! Ow!
(steady gliss.)
Gtr. II
Gtr. II
A.H.
(15ma)
Full
w/o slide
A.H.
(15ma)
H Full Full Full
A.H. pitches: F#
A.H.
(15ma)
Full Full
semi-
harm.
Full Full
A.H.
sl.
TP H TP 1/2 TP H TP P H P sl. sl. H P TP P sl. H P TP
A.H. pitch: B

189

A.H.
(15ma)
A.H.
(15ma)
Full
1/2
sl.
T P
T P
Full
P
hold bend
hold bend
hold bend
3
3
A.H. pitches: F#
A C# B
Full
A.H.
(15ma)
3
A.H.
(15ma)
sl.
2
P
Full
1/2
P H
P H
rake
Full
A.H.
A.H.
sl.
A.H. pitches: D E
(F# pedal)
B C#
A B
F#
E F# E F#
A
(A pedal)
*Gtr. I
sl.
sl.
sl.
*2½
P 3/4 Full
T 2½
1/2
T
P
P
sl. sl.
Full
Full
Full
1/2 P Full
sl. sl. sl.
sl.
rake
(F# pedal) *All bends generated from left hand.
*w/Slide.
(B pedal)
F# pedal
B C#
A B
F#
E (type 2)
3
D
1/2
1½ 1½
1/2
Full Full Full
P
3
3
3
(A pedal)
E F# E F#
A
(F# pedal)
B C#
A B
C#
C#sus4
(B pedal)
sl.
Full
Full
1/2 Full
Full Full Full 1/2 Full
T P T P
sl. sl.
(steady gliss.)
sl.
sl.

F#m7
E B A5 B5
F#m7(sus4)
Gtr. II
Full
Full
sl. sl. P
1/4 1/2 Full
1/2 Full
3
3 3
Full
T P H T P H
trem. bar
(steady gliss.)
semi-harm.
semi-harm.
sl. P
trem. bar
Gtr. I
P
sl.
sl.
sl.
sl. P
E
B
N.C.
Pre-chorus
C#5
I've   been   out ____ there, ____________
8va
TPH TPH TPH TPH TP TP TP TPP
sl. H TP TP
Full
grad. bend
dim.
P

D5 A5 E5 B5 N.C. C# D A Esus4 E N.C.
try'n'_ a bit of ev-'ry-thing,_ ah!
But it's all
Gtr. I
P.M.------|
P.M.------|
C#
sex with-out_ love!______
D5 A5 E5 B5 N.C. C#
I found_the real_ thing is Pound-cake.
P.M.------|
B7sus4 N.C. A Chorus E5
Home______ grown_ an' down_
Gtr. III (12-stg. elec.)------------
Gtrs. I & II
(clean tone)
H P
sl.
D5 D6/9(no 3rd) Aadd9/C# N.C.
_ home, yeah, that's a wom-an._____
Still
* P
Harm.------------
(8va)
sl.
(w/slap-back echo------------
Harm.------------
sl.
*Two gtrs. One gtr. allows chords to sustain while other
plays harmonics.

E5
D5 D6/9(no 3rd)
Aadd9/C#
N.C.
cook - in' with that old time, long lost rec - i - pe,___ yeah!__ Woo!__
Harm.
(8va)
P
sl.
sl.
sl.
sl.
w/Fill 1
E5
D5 D6/9(no 3rd)
She's down___ home_ an' down___ home. Ow,___
Harm.
(8va)
trem. bar
1/2
1/2
Harm.
sl.
Aadd9/C#
w/Fills 2 & 3
w/Rhy. Fig. 1 (2 times)
(E pedal)
A B   G A   E
that's my wom - an!__ Gim - me some - a that Uh,__ a, huh,__ huh!__
Gtr. II
A.H.
(15ma)
sl.
A.H.
A.H. pitch: G
Fill 1
Harm.
(8va)
1½
trem. bar
1½
Harm.
Fill 2
1½
Harm.
(8va)
2½ 1½
trem. bar
1½ Harm.
2½ 1½
Fill 3
Harm.
(8va)
1/2
1 1½ 2½ 4½
trem. bar
Harm.
1½
1/2
1 1½ 2½ 4½
12

(A pedal)
DE DE G
A B G A E D C
Uh, a, huh, huh!
Lem-me on there!
A.H. (15ma) Full
Full A.H. (15ma) Full
A.H. pitches: B B
(E pedal)
A B G A E DE DE G
(A pedal)
A B G A E
Uh, a, huh, huh! Uh! Uh, a, huh, huh,
Full A.H. (15ma)
P.M. A.H.
D G C
Out chorus
E5
well! Home grown an' down
Full Full Full Full Full 1½ Full
Gtr. II
Full P Full P Full Full Full 1½ Full
Rhy. Fig. 2
Gtr. I

194

D6/9(no 3rd)
Aadd9/C#
home, woo! Come on, babe!
8va
Full
1/2 Full
Full
loco 3
Full
1/2 Full
Full
sl.
sl.
(14) (14) 3
sl.
22
(22) 22 22 22
(22)
sl.
19
20
12 12 14
P
sl.
P
sl.
0 0 0 0
0 0
0
0 0 0 0
9 7 7 7 7
7 7
7 6 6 6 6
6 6
9 7 7 7 7
7 7
7 7 7 7 7
7 7
7 5 5 5 5
5 5
5 4 4 4 4
4 4
sl.
sl.
w/Rhy. Fig. 2 (till fade)
E5
Gim-me some-a that, gim-me some-a that... Home grown, way down
1/2 Full
Full
sl.
sl.
sl.
sl.
sl.
sl.
3
3
1/2 Full
Full
sl. sl.
sl.
sl.
sl.
12 15 (15)
(15)
21
(21) 6
21
(21) 4
21
12 14
12 14
(end Rhy. Fig. 2)

D6/9(no 3rd)
Aadd9/C#
home! Yeah! No!
Full 2 Full 1/2
P.M. Full 2 Full 1/2
1/2 Full Full
E5
D6/9(no 3rd)
Begin fade
Aadd9/C#
Uh, a, huh, huh! Yeah! Gim - me some - a that... Woo!
Full 1/2
E5
D6/9(no 3rd)
C'-mon, babe!
8va
loco
H TP TP TP P
Aadd9/C#
E5
Fade out
Oh, no, oh, no, no, oh, woo! Uh, huh, huh!
8va
H T sl. T P P H H TP P T 1/2 P 1/2 Full
Full Full Full

TOP OF THE WORLD

Words and Music by
Edward Van Halen, Alex Van Halen,
Michael Anthony and Sammy Hagar

197

N.C.(B5)
E5
1st Verse
A
I know you be - lieve in me.
(Gtr. II out)
Full
Full
Full
Full
P
P
Rhy. Fig. 1
w/fingers
E
N.C.
E5
That's all I ev - er need.
Uh - huh.
No, no, noth-
sl.
sl.
sl.
sl.
A
E
ing's gon - na stop it. Noth - in' will es - cape me.
Oh, no.
sl.
sl.

C#5
B5
A5
Pre-chorus
A
B/A E/A
B
A
N.C.
Hey,________ ba - by.
Yeah, it's the on - ly way out.__
(end Rhy. Fig. 1)
Rhy. Fig. 2
w/pick
P.M.
P.M. P.M.
Esus4 E D
E/D Esus4/D
E/D
D
Oh,________ lit - tle dar__ lin',
now come on,__ what's it all a - bout?
P.M.
P.M. P.M.
P.M.
pick slide
N.C.
E
Chorus
B
E A
E/A B
E
B E
Stand - in' on top__ of__ the world__
for a lit - tle__
(end Rhy. Fig. 2)
Rhy. Fig. 3
P.M.
P.M.--- P.M.
P.M.--- P.M.
sl.
sl.
N.C.
E5
B
E A
E/A B
E
B E
__ while. Stand - in' on top__ of__ the world.__
Gon - na give__
(end Rhy. Fig. 3)
P.M. P.M.
P.M.--- P.M.
P.M.--- P.M.
sl.
sl.

Bsus4   B   A5   Asus2   2nd Verse w/Rhy. Fig. 1   E5   A
it all ____ we've got. ____   Oh ____ no, ____ I wan-na touch. I've got ____

E   N.C.   E5   A
to have a lit-tle taste. ____   I just wan-na sink my teeth in that fine ____
Gtr. II   A.H. (8va)   *Tapped harmonics.   Full   Full   Full
Full   *T   T   T   T
*Tapped harmonics.

E   C#5   B5   Pre-chorus w/Rhy. Fig. 2   A5   A
piece of real es-tate. ____   Yeah. ____   Hey, ____ ba-
pick slide

B/A   E/A   B   A   N.C.   Esus4   E   D
by.   Whoo!   Make it nice ____ and sweet. ____   Mm.   Oh, ____ lit-tle dar-
Full   Full   P
P.M.

Chorus
w/Rhy. Fig. 3
E/D Esus4/D E/D D N.C. E B E A
lin', let's take a walk down Eas-y Street. Stand - in' on top
Full
8va
Full
(9) (9) 17 (17) 17 (17) 17 14 17 17

E/A B E B E N.C. E5 B E A
of the world for a lit-tle while. Stand - in' on top
8va
1/2
1/2
(17) 17 17 (17) 17 14 16 16 (16) 16 14 17 (17) 17 14 17 17
14 16 16 14

E/A B E B E Gtr. D5 A5(cont. in Bridge G/B Csus2 Dsus2
I notation)
of the world. Let's give it all we've got. (Oo, oo, oo. Ba-
(Gtr. II out)
8va
Full Gtr. loco
I
Full let ring
(17) 17 17 (17) 17 14 19 (19) 22 3 3 3
14 16 16 14 2 3 0

G/B Csus2 G5 G/B Csus2 D5
by, got-ta feel it. Oh, wan-na touch it now.
Oo, oo. Oo, oo, oo. Oo, oo, oo,
(0) 2 3 3 3 3 3 2 0 (3) 3 3
0 0 (3) 3 3 0
3 2 3 3 2 3

201

Em
F#m
G5
A5
B5
E5
See the whole wide world turn upside down.
oo.
Oo,
oo.
Oo,
oo.)
*8va
Full
Gtr. II
Gtr. I
Full
sl.
(Gtr. I cont. in slashes)
*8va applies to Gtr. II only.
Guitar solo
Gtr. I
loco
(Gtr. II)
w/wah
sl. sl,
1/4
C5
sl.
1/4
sl.
D5
E5
sl.
C5
A.H.
(8va)
sl. sl.
sl. sl.
A.H.
sl.
sl.
A.H. pitch: A
open
E
sl,
D5
(cont. in notation)
8va
sl. sl.
6
sl.
(wah off)
sl. sl.
sl.

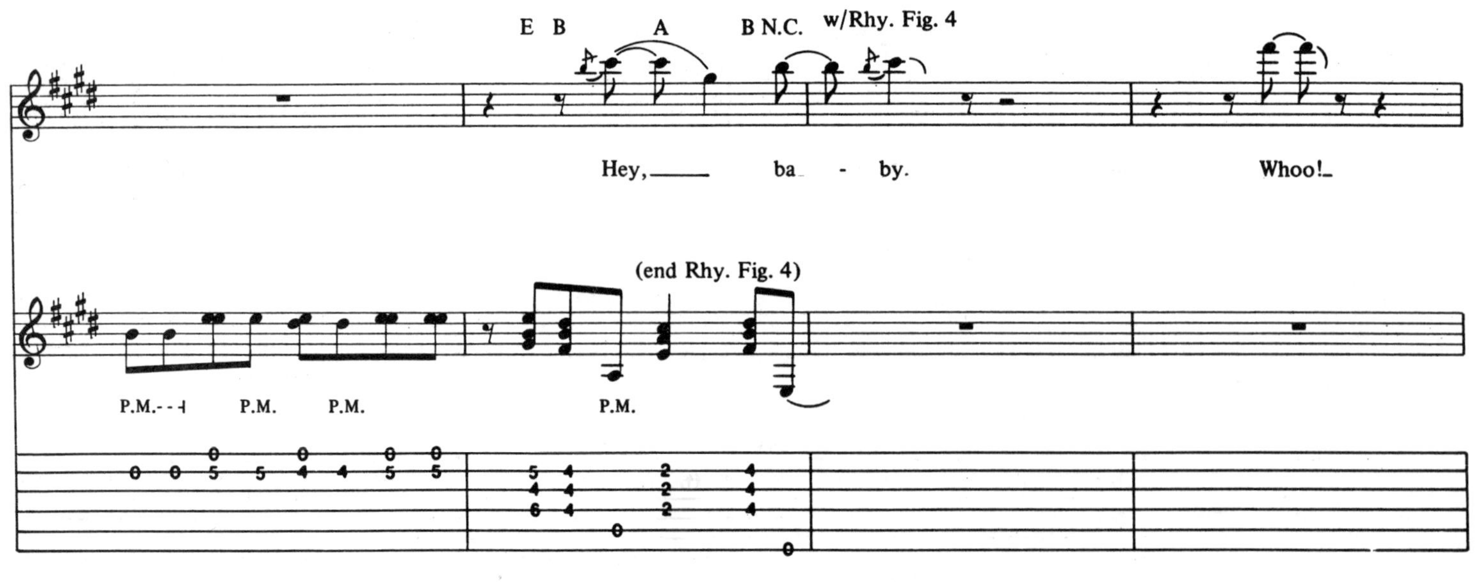

E B   A   B N.C.   w/Rhy. Fig. 4
Hey,____ ba - by.
Whoo!_
(end Rhy. Fig. 4)
P.M.--| P.M.   P.M.
P.M.

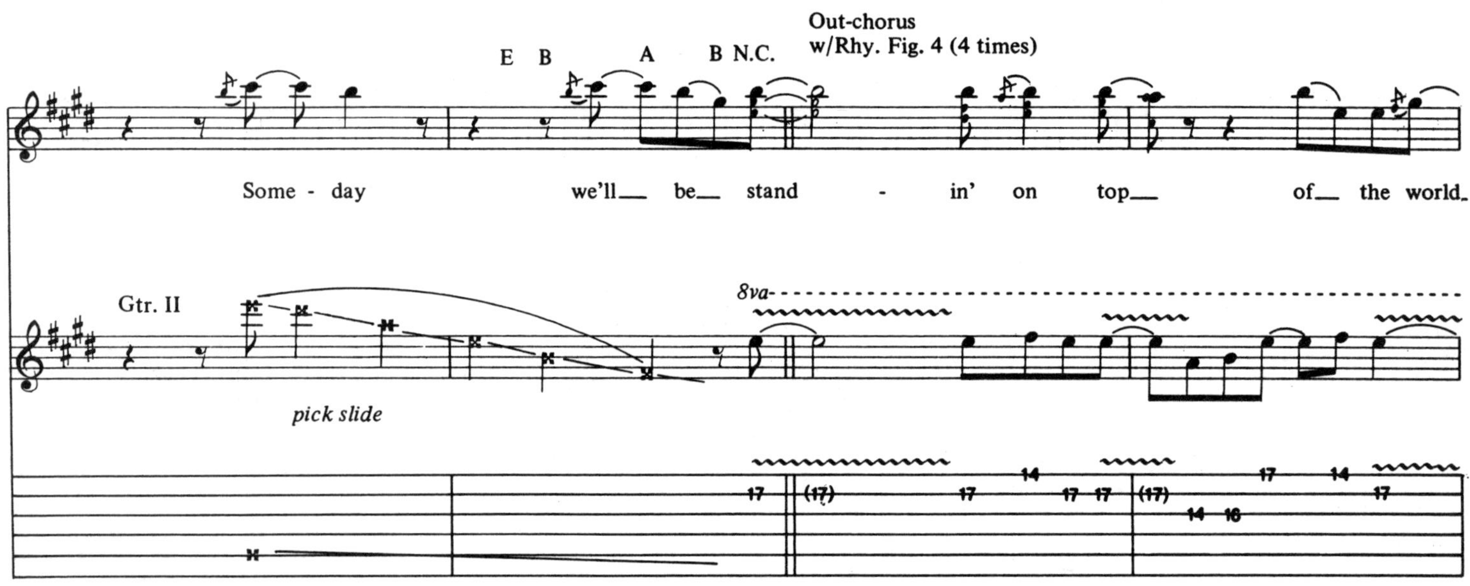

E   B   A   B N.C.
Out-chorus
w/Rhy. Fig. 4 (4 times)
Some - day   we'll__ be__ stand - in' on top__   of__ the world.
Gtr. II
pick slide
8va-

E B   A   B N.C.
___ for a lit - tle__ while.   Stand - in' on top__   of__ the world__
8va-
Full   Full   Full   2
Full   Full   Full   2

E B A B N.C.
till we__ can't stop.__ Stand - in on__ top__ of__ the world__
8va-
Full Full 2
Full Full 2
(17) 17 16 17 17 (17) (17) 17 14 17 17 (17) 17 14 17
14 18 14 16

E B A B N.C.
for a lit - tle__ while.__ Stand - in' on top__ of__ the world..
8va-
H T TP TP TP 1/2 T
H T TP TP TP 1/2 T
(17) 17 17 (17) 12 17 11 17 10 17 8 17 17 14 17 17 (17) 17 14 17
14 18 14 16

w/Rhy. Fig. 3 (1st 4 bars only) (till end)
E B A B E B E A E/A B E
Gon -na give__ it all__ we've got.__ Hey,__ ba-
(Stand - in' on top.)__
8va-
Full Full 2
Full Full 2
(17) 17 14 17 (17) 17 (17) (17) 17 14 17 17 (17) 17 14 17
14 18 14 16

Begin fade
B E N.C. E B E A E/A B E
by.
Stand - in' on top.)
Hey, dar -
8va
Full 2
(17) 17 17 (17) 17 17 17 17 (17) 17 14 17 17 (17) 17 14 17
18 14 16
14
B E N.C. E B E A
lin'. Whoo! Stand - in' on top.
8va
Full Full 2
(17) 17 14 17 17 (17) (17) (17) 17 14 17 17
18 14
14
Fade out
E/A B E B E N.C. E
Stand - in' on top.
Stand-
8va
H T P T P T P 1/2 T
(17) 17 14 17 (17) 17 17 (17) 12 17 11 17 10 17 8 17 17
14 16 16
14

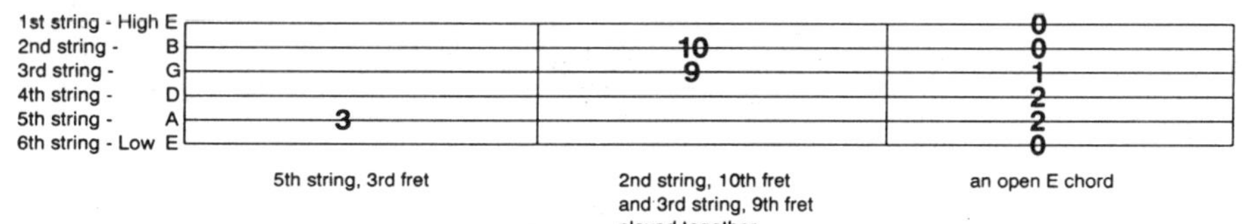
• TABLATURE EXPLANATION/NOTATION LEGEND •

TABLATURE: A six-line staff that graphically represents the guitar fingerboard. By placing a number on the appropriate line, the string and fret of any note can be indicated. For example:

1st string - High E
2nd string - B
3rd string - G
4th string - D
5th string - A
6th string - Low E

5th string, 3rd fret

2nd string, 10th fret
and 3rd string, 9th fret
played together

an open E chord

Definitions for Special Guitar Notation

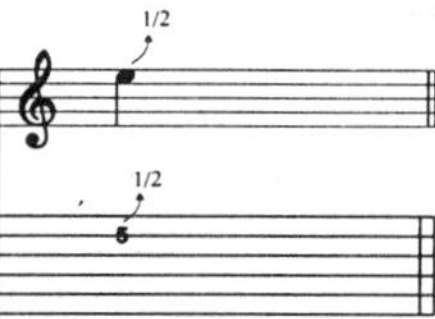
BEND: Strike the note and bend up ½ step (one fret).

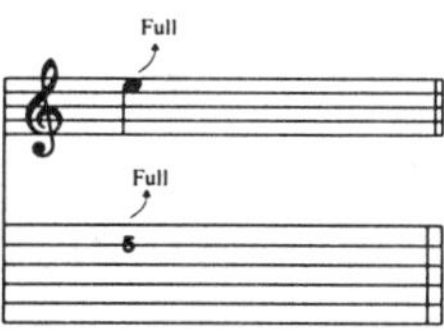
BEND: Strike the note and bend up a whole step (two frets).

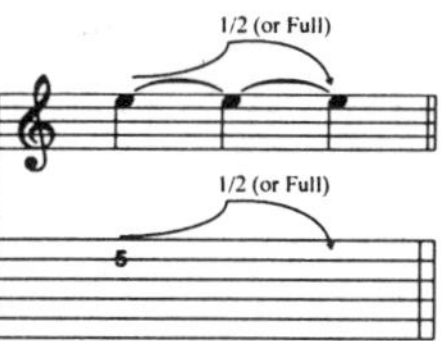
BEND AND RELEASE: Strike the note and bend up ½ (or whole) step, then release the bend back to the original note. All three notes are tied; only the first note is struck.

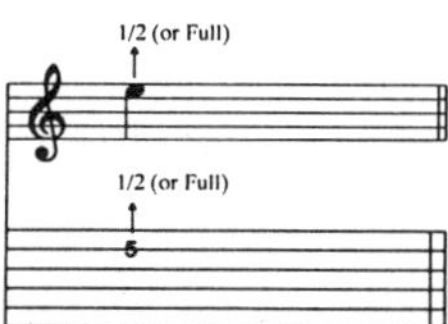
PRE-BEND: Bend the note up ½ (or whole) step, then strike it.

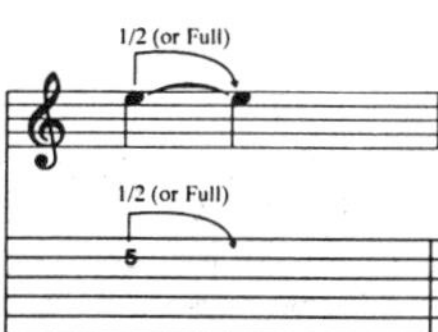
PRE-BEND AND RELEASE: Bend the note up ½ (or whole) step, strike it and release the bend back to the original note.

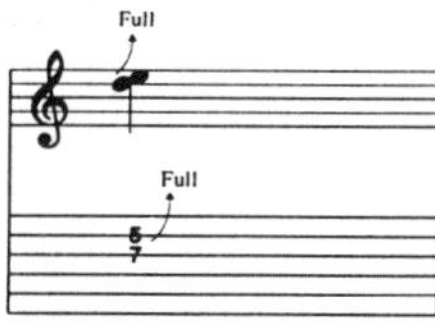
UNISON BEND: Strike the two notes simultaneously and bend the lower note to the pitch of the higher.

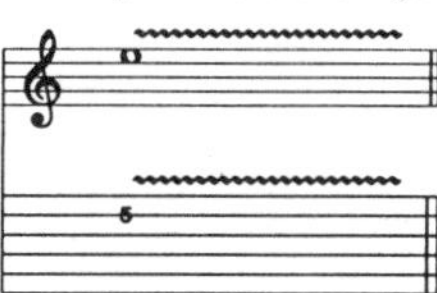
VIBRATO: Vibrate the note by rapidly bending and releasing the string with a left-hand finger.

WIDE OR EXAGGERATED VIBRATO: Vibrate the pitch to a greater degree with a left-hand finger or the tremolo bar.

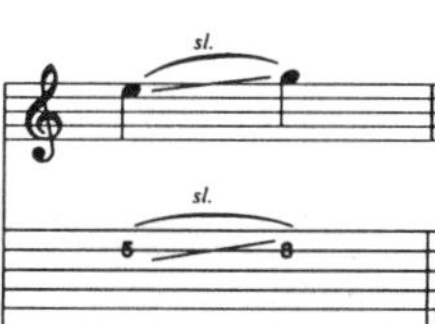
SLIDE: Strike the first note and then with the same left-hand finger move up the string to the second note. The second note is not struck.

SLIDE: Same as above, except the second note is struck.

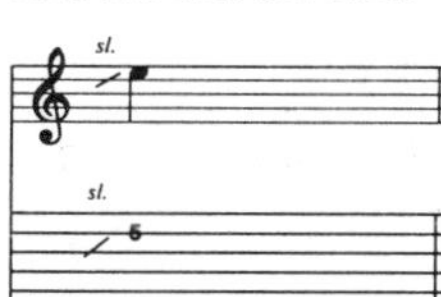
SLIDE: Slide up to the note indicated from a few frets below.

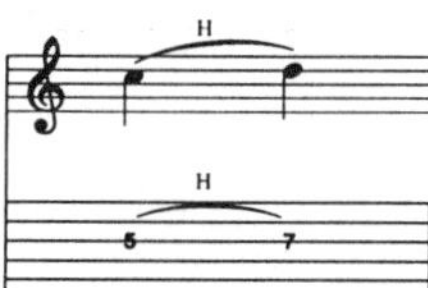
HAMMER-ON: Strike the first (lower) note, then sound the higher note with another finger by fretting it without picking.

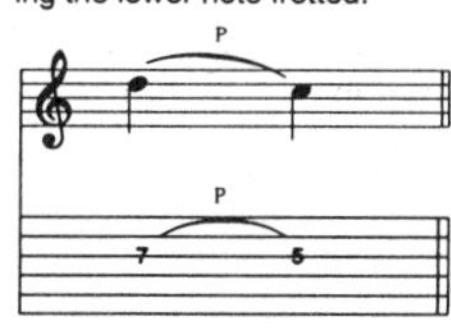
PULL-OFF: Place both fingers on the notes to be sounded. Strike the first (higher) note, then sound the lower note by pulling the finger off the higher note while keeping the lower note fretted.

TRILL: Very rapidly alternate between the note indicated and the small note shown in parentheses by hammering on and pulling off.

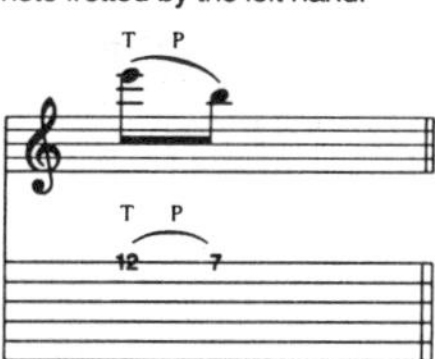
TAPPING: Hammer ("tap") the fret indicated with the right-hand index or middle finger and pull off to the note fretted by the left hand.

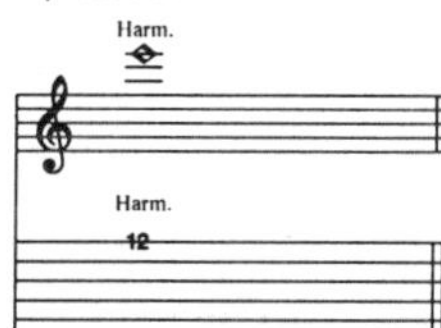
NATURAL HARMONIC: With a left-hand finger, lightly touch the string over the fret indicated, then strike it. A chime-like sound is produced.

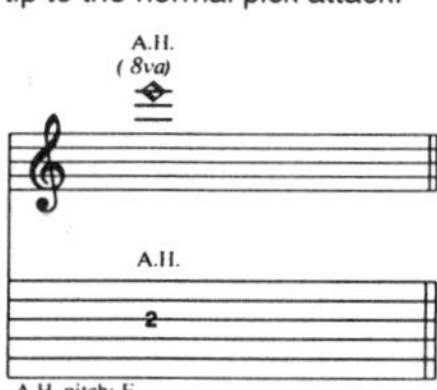
ARTIFICIAL HARMONIC: Fret the note normally and sound the harmonic by adding the right-hand thumb edge or index finger tip to the normal pick attack.

A.H. pitch: E

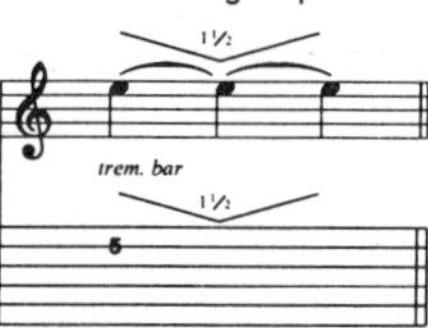
TREMOLO BAR: Drop the note by the number of steps indicated, then return to original pitch.

PALM MUTE: With the right hand, partially mute the note by lightly touching the string just before the bridge.

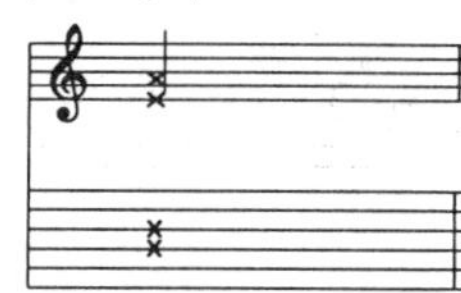
MUFFLED STRINGS: Lay the left hand across the strings without depressing them to the fret-board; strike the strings with the right hand, producing a percussive sound.

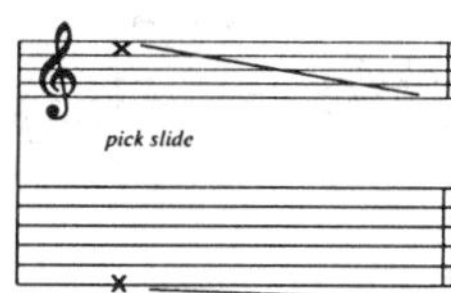
PICK SLIDE: Rub the pick edge down the length of the string to produce a scratchy sound.

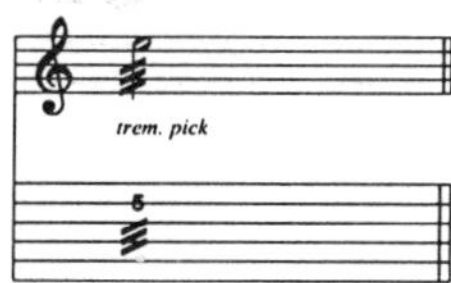
TREMOLO PICKING: Pick the note as rapidly and continuously as possible.

RHYTHM SLASHES: Strum chords in rhythm indicated. Use chord voicings found in the fingering diagrams at the top of the first page of the transcription.

SINGLE-NOTE RHYTHM SLASHES: The circled number above the note name indicates which string to play. When successive notes are played on the same string, only the fret numbers are given.